Upland Game Bird Cookery

Eileen Clarke

Ducks Unlimited, Inc.
Memphis, Tennessee

Ducks Unlimited, Inc., and colophon are registered trademarks of Ducks Unlimited, Inc.

Published by Ducks Unlimited, Inc.
John A. Tomke, President
Julius Wall, Chairman of the Board
D. A. (Don) Young, Executive Vice President

Edited by Doug Truax
Designed by Karen Almand

ISBN: 1-932052-09-7

Published May 2003

DUCKS UNLIMITED, INC.
Ducks Unlimited conserves, restores, and manages wetlands and associated habitats for North America's waterfowl. These habitats also benefit other wildlife and people. Since its founding in 1937, DU has raised more than $1.6 billion, which has contributed to the conservation of over 10 million acres of prime wildlife habitat in all fifty states, each of the Canadian provinces, and in key areas of Mexico. In the U.S. alone, DU has helped to conserve over 2 million acres of waterfowl habitat. Some 900 species of wildlife live and flourish on DU projects, including many threatened and endangered species.

Library of Congress Cataloging-in-Publication Data

Clarke, Eileen.
  Upland game bird cookery / Eileen Clarke.
    p. cm.
ISBN 1-932052-09-7 (alk. paper)
1. Cookery (Poultry) 2. Cookery (Game) 3. Upland game birds. I.
Title.
  TX750.C57 2003
  641.6'91--dc21
                        2003008070

Call to Action

The success of Ducks Unlimited hinges upon each member's personal involvement in the conservation of North America's wetlands and waterfowl. You can help Ducks Unlimited meet its conservation goals by volunteering your time, energy, and resources; by participating in our conservation programs; and by encouraging others to do the same. To learn more about how you can make a difference for the ducks, call 1-800-45-DUCKS.

Table of Contents

Table of Contents

Table of Contents

Table of Contents

Table of Contents

**To Thomas Haviland—at 16, the most avid hunter I know—
with the wish that you always have that desire and the wild open spaces to fulfill it**

Acknowledgments

My thanks to the many people who have shared their recipes, time, and hunting camps to make this book possible. Special thanks to:

Cam Wyly, owner of Wyly Pheasant Farm and Ranch, Aberdeen, South Dakota, for his abundant pheasants, but not for teaching my dog to expect sugar-glazed donut holes at his lunch break.

Uncle Buck's Lodge, Brewster, Nebraska, in the heart of the Sandhills and a great pheasant and prairie chicken hunting destination, and Mike Clark, upland bird guide and wily dog handler and breeder, for trying to help me get a leg up on my husband, John, who's been hunting a lot longer than I have and always seems to have the birds fly in front of him.

Winchester Ammunition, for their high-velocity pheasant loads that let this toe-shooter get a better lead on those fast-flying birds.

Browning Arms, for their straight-shooting auto 20-gauge that made having fun in the field a lot more fun.

White Oak Plantation, always, both for their Scalloped Pineapple and their ability to make turkeys act just stupid enough, just often enough.

Richard Beebe and Curt Nelson, of Redding Reloading Equipment, for making turkeys do all the things they're not supposed to do—including walk on water. And for their fine turkey recipes.

Finally, the biggest debt is to those friends who hunted with me, then donated their own birds to the book: Doug Phair, for his hard-won doves in early September's 100°F temperatures; Gayle and John Haviland, for sharing their secret hunting spot—and their delicate blues; and Randy Havel and his grouse camp partners, who'd been sharing adventures for twenty-five years and invited me into camp, then were kind enough to toss all their woodcock into my cooler.

Introduction

Ionce knew a bird hunter who dedicated his life to hunting only one species of bird, refusing to shoot the odd Hungarian partridge or sharp-tailed grouse that jumped up from the "wrong" cover. Most of us, however, are human. As we walk the fields and mountains of bird cover, we're grateful for every bird that flushes at our feet, every fowl that miscalculates its margin of safety, and every classy retrieve that our faithful companion manages to complete. Indeed, the mixed bag of bird hunting is part of the joy of our days afield. But for the cook that same mixed bag can be a problem. From the delicate white meat of a ruffed grouse to the at times all-but-unpalatable wild-running birds of the prairies, no other single pursuit brings such different flavors to the kitchen, or spans quite as wide a variety of weather and climate conditions as upland bird hunting. Just try to cool a brace of doves down properly in early September, or to keep one precious late-season pheasant from freezing before you get it home.

Age of the bird, its sex, state of mind, what it has eaten, and weather all affect tenderness and taste—before you ever shoulder your gun. Then field care and the ride home add their distinctive touch. You might not know right away what you have, but sometime in April, when you thaw out a few birds from the freezer, you might start wondering how hard it would really be to hunt only in lush feed lots. Or how difficult it might be to evaluate fat content and the bird's age, on the wing, before you shot.

Relax. A little care in the field goes a long way toward solving the problems of Mother Nature, and even if the worst has happened, there are ways to repair the damage. In these pages I'll share techniques I've learned over the years through trial and error, and the recipes and tips fellow hunters have shared with me. From salt soaks to marinades, dry rubs to moist-cooking, flavor injections to cutting board magic, all will ease your anxiety and make cooking less stressful and more tasty than you thought possible.

The Gist of the Matter: What Does It Taste Like ? How Many Should I Cook ? When Is It Done ?

In this cookbook the recipes have been grouped according the shade of each bird's flesh, starting with the mild, pale-meated birds up front and ending with the dark-meated birds. (Except for turkey, which is in a class by itself because of its size.) I've done this because color isn't arbitrary. And while some would argue that woodcock would be an exception, for the most part color is a very good indicator of taste. As long as good field-care technique was used, and Mother Nature cooperated just a bit, pale flesh does translate into mild flavor. Thus you'll notice fewer marinades and milder ingredients in the front of the book, and more intense flavors and more fixing-up in the back.

This structure allows you to mix and match recipes with like-tasting birds depending on what you have the most of in your freezer and what ingredients you enjoy. I've cooked quail with my favorite grouse ingredients (in years when grouse weren't on the agenda), and there's no reason you can't use pheasant with the ingredients for a chukar recipe, sharp-tailed grouse with a prairie chicken recipe, or sage grouse with either. Just maintain the ratio of meat to other ingredients.

How Many Should I Cook ?

The U.S. Department of Agriculture recommends 4 ounces of meat per serving, one serving of meat per day for healthy men, women, and children. Most men eat more than that, and most women, as a rule, eat less. If you've got a teenage boy, he's probably protein loading, eating perhaps 2 to 3 times the recommended allowance. So calculate how much protein your family eats per meal, and you'll quickly know how many birds to cook.

The smallest upland game birds are dove and woodcock, which have a dressed weight of 2 to 4 ounces each, with doves usually on the lighter end. Quail dress out at about 4 ounces each. Depending on age, food, and time of year, all of these small upland birds can vary an ounce or two either way.

A little larger are Hungarian partridge, which dress out at 7 to 10 ounces. Chukar, at 10 to 12 ounces, are slightly larger than Huns, and ruffed and Spruce (or Franklin) grouse are a few ounces heavier still.

Sharp-tailed grouse and prairie chickens are very similar in appearance and food habits, and not surprisingly, they are also comparable in size and taste. Sharptails range from about 1 to 1¼ pounds, while prairie chickens are slightly larger, ranging from 1¼ to 1½ pounds. (Individual birds of this size can vary several ounces either way. In general, the larger the species the more variable the size from bird to bird.)

Then come pheasants and blue grouse, at 1½ to 1¾ pounds. Sage grouse are the largest of our wing-shot birds, and also vary the most in weight. Right now I have 3 sage grouse in my freezer that weigh from 1¾ pounds to 3 pounds. And a couple of years ago, my husband and I had a bird that weighed 5 pounds, plucked and ready for the oven.

Turkeys vary the most in size, from jakes that are as small and light as a large sage grouse, to Missouri boss gobblers that tip the scales at 25 pounds plus. A more normal weight for a mature adult with easily discernible beard is 12–18 pounds.

All these weights are for whole birds—plucked and cleaned and ready to go in the oven. Of that weight, about half is edible. A dressed 1-pound game bird will yield about 5-6 ounces of breast meat and 1½ to 2 ounces of leg meat. Likewise, a 4-ounce bird will yield 1½ ounces boned breast meat and ¾ ounce leg meat. (Oddly, the ratio stays the same no matter the size of the bird.) For recipes that use the breast only, figure it to be about ⅓ of the total weight of the cleaned bird.

In the real world, this means that a small, 1-pound pheasant will yield 2 servings (four ounces of meat per serving). A fully mature rooster, weighing close to 2 pounds, may feed four.

For small birds, like dove and woodcock, you need to allow two to three whole birds per person. And whole is the way to eat these small birds. It's a lot more fun to gnaw the meat off the bones than to cut it off, and you waste less.

Which Birds Can Be Quick Grilled ?
Which Can Be Slow Roasted ?

If you've been fortunate enough to bring home more than one pheasant (or more than one bird of any other species), it's helpful after you've cleaned the birds to arrange them on the counter according to size. The smaller birds of each species will generally be more suitable for dishes calling for quick cooking. They're likely to be younger birds, which usually means their flesh will be more tender. The larger birds of each species are likely to be older. That doesn't mean the mature birds will necessarily be tough—only that the younger birds will be more tender, more mild, more able to pass muster when cooked hot and quick, like on the barbecue. Now check the birds again: If there's one that's noticeably larger than the others, or one whose flesh looks darker and more dense, make a note on the freezer wrap that it should be cooked slow and moist.

When is it done? My friend Josh Turner sent me the perfect bird recipe the other day—Popcorn Stuffed Pheasant. You bake the bird in a 350°F oven, brush it lavishly with herbed butter, and when the popcorn blows the oven door open and the pheasant flies across the room, it's done. Ah, if it were only that easy.

I like to cook *wild* birds until the flesh is just past pink and no further. That's about 150°F on a meat thermometer when you check the bird in the oven or barbecue. A whole bird will actually continue cooking for another 8–10 minutes, which means it reaches a peak of about 160°F.

Birds that come from game preserves—and birds that have been in close contact with each other for whatever reason—are another story. Such birds need to be cooked to 175°F. (Stick a meat thermometer in the thigh—without touching bone.) When you add in that 8–10 degrees of "counter cooking" you'll be at a safe 183°F–185°F. Why the higher temperature? Preserve birds are exposed to a lot more bugs than wild birds. Don't believe me? Think of your local elementary school—in cold and flu season. Birds kept in such close quarters need to be cooked thoroughly. To make up for the loss of internal moisture, baste them more when cooking, or choose a moist-cooking recipe in the first place, so you still end up with a tender, delicious bird.

Chapter One

Ruffed, Blue, and Franklin Grouse

Easiest Grilled Ruffed Grouse Breast

serves 4

Ingredients

FOR THE GROUSE

4 tablespoons oil
Juice of 1 lemon
4 bay leaves
¼ teaspoon black pepper
Boned breasts of 2 ruffed grouse

FOR THE VEGETABLES

2 tablespoons oil
1 tablespoon onion flakes
1 elephant garlic (a large, milder variety of garlic), sliced thin
1 teaspoon garlic salt
2 roma or plum tomatoes, halved
1 green pepper, quartered
1 yellow onion, sliced thick, lengthwise—root to stem
2 hinged grates (the kind used to cook burgers)

Hot weather getting you down? Don't want to cook? Let's make dinner incredibly easy. We'll take a spice you've had in your cupboard for years and use it in a way you have probably never used it before. Then we'll throw some vegetables on the grill, too. Because this is dinner, and you're going to make your family smile.

PREPARATION

1. In the blender, combine the oil, lemon, bay leaves, and black pepper. Purée until the bay leaves are well minced but not liquefied.
2. Pour the marinade into a resealable plastic bag or a bowl, and add the grouse. Seal or cover and refrigerate 1-2 hours.
3. Combine the oil, onion flakes, and garlic salt for the veggies and let sit.

COOKING

1. Preheat the barbecue to medium heat. Remove the grouse breasts from the marinade and let sit at room temperature for 10 to 15 minutes before grilling.
2. Since the tomatoes cook faster than the peppers and onions, place the sliced onions and peppers on the first grate. Place the halves of tomatoes on the second grate. Arrange the garlic slices on top of all the vegetables and

brush with the seasoned oil. Now start the onions and peppers.

3. When the onions and peppers start getting soft, in about 5 to 7 minutes, start the tomatoes and place the grouse breasts on the grill. Cook both the tomatoes and grouse about 3–4 minutes to a side. Lightly brown on the outside but don't overcook on the inside. The grilling goes very fast, so if you want salad on the side, have it on the table before you start grilling. ⊛

Tip

Since ruffed and spruce grouse are the same size, have the same pale flesh, and generally have the same eating habits, any ruffed grouse recipe can be used for spruce grouse. You can substitute blue grouse, as well, but you'll have to adjust cooking time and the other ingredients because blues are almost twice as big as ruffed and spruce grouse. Be aware that, in late fall, spruce and blue grouse are liable to switch from eating tender aspen buds to conifers. If your season runs that long, you may want to lay off the conifer-eaters and concentrate on ruffed grouse for table fare.

Simply Succulent Roast Ruffed

serves 2

Ingredients

2 tablespoons softened butter
⅛ teaspoon salt
⅛ teaspoon coarse ground black pepper
1 whole ruffed grouse, skin on (about 12 ounces)

The number one complaint about wild birds? They're dry. Number one mistake? Cooking them too long. How do you avoid these problems? Baste with butter. And don't cook wild birds to the internal temperature of 170° to 180°F recommended for commercially raised birds. I don't know why, but when I cook chicken to 150°F it's half raw and running red. When I do the same with ruffed grouse, there is no pink, no raw meat, and no problem. At 150°F, with a butter baste, the ruffed grouse is succulent all the way down to its toenails.

COOKING

1. Preheat the oven to 350°F. In a cup, combine the butter with the salt and pepper. Set aside.
2. Check your grouse: Trim off any rough edges and rinse the bird inside and out. Pluck any stray feathers and dry the bird inside and out with paper towels.
3. Place the bird in a small open roasting pan (or cast-iron skillet). If you have a rack, place that inside the roasting pan first, so the bird sits up out of the drippings.
4. Brush or rub the bird with the seasoned butter and place in the oven. Set your timer to go off every 10 minutes, and baste until a meat thermometer, placed in the thickest part of the thigh, reads 150°F. This 12-ounce bird will take about 40 minutes. Do not overcook.
5. Remove the bird from the oven immediately and place the pan, rack, and bird on the counter to cool 10 minutes. Carve and arrange the legs and breast on a platter, pouring the pan juices over the meat. Serve with baked potatoes and Brussels sprouts. ❁

Roast Crispy Ruffed Grouse

recipe on page 5

Shot Shell Soup

recipe on page 7

America's Team
Baked Ruffed Grouse

recipe on page 8

Mountain Lunch

recipe on page 13

Quail Bobs with Peanut Sauce

recipe on page 20

A Braised Brace
of Quail

recipe on page 23

Quail Cacciatore

recipe on page 26

Citrus Quail

recipe on page 24

White-On-White Chili

recipe on page 30

Quail Empanadas

recipe on page 25

Pheasant Poppers

recipe on page 42

Chinese
Waldorf Salad

recipe on page 44

Teriyaki Kabobs with Wasabi Dipping Sauce

recipe on page 40

Grilled Pheasant Breast with Apricot-Kumquat Salsa

recipe on page 34

Poached
Pheasant Salad

recipe on page 45

Hot Ginger
Pheasant Soup

recipe on page 47

Rubbed Pheasant

recipe on page 50

Pheasant
Peasant Pie

recipe on page 49

Wily Rooster Pot Roast

recipe on page 53

Tortilla Soup

recipe on page 46

Traditional Marinated
Roast Pheasant

recipe on page 52

South American Hoagie

recipe on page 55

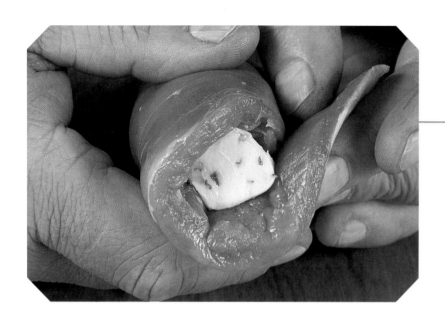

Pheasant Kiev

recipe on page 54

Heavenly Penne
Casserole

recipe on page 56

Roast Crispy Ruffed Grouse

serves 1–2

Ingredients

2 tablespoons softened butter
3 tablespoons minced parsley
1 teaspoon chopped chives
1 clove garlic, minced
1 whole ruffed grouse, skin on

The one drawback to the Simply Succulent Roast Grouse recipe is that you don't get a crisp, brown breast. If you're willing to give up just a bit of the juiciness and want a browned bird, try this roasting recipe. But I warn you: this one is more work. With the high initial heat, you need to turn the bird during cooking to keep the breast from getting too dry.

COOKING

1. Preheat the oven to 450°F. In a cup, combine the butter, parsley, chives, and garlic. Set it aside.
2. Check your grouse: Trim off any rough edges; rinse the bird inside and out; pluck any stray feathers; and dry the bird inside and out with paper towels.
3. Place the bird in a small open roasting pan (or cast-iron skillet). If you have a rack, place that inside the roasting pan first to raise the bird out of the drippings.
4. Brush or rub the bird with the herbed butter, and place it in the center of the oven. Roast for 15 minutes, then turn the bird on its side, baste with the pan drippings, and lower the heat to 350°F.
5. Roast another 10 minutes. Turn the bird to the other side, and baste with the pan drippings. In 10 more minutes, turn the bird breast up, baste one more time, and roast 10 more minutes for a total of 45 minutes. A meat thermometer placed in the thickest part of the thigh should measure 150°F. Remove the pan from the oven, and allow the bird to sit for 10 minutes before carving. Serve hot with mashed potatoes and pan juices over all, or cold with a good peach chutney. ◉

Low-Fat Dry-Roasted Ruffed Grouse

serves 2

Ingredients

1 tablespoon olive oil
¼ teaspoon minced fresh sage leaves
¼ teaspoon salt
⅛ teaspoon pepper
1 whole ruffed grouse

For those watching their waistlines or their cholesterol, olive oil is only slightly less spectacular at keeping birds moist as that revered old Mr. Healthy himself, butter. The trick is to baste the bird often (as in every 10 minutes) with whatever pan juices you have—and of course not overcook it. (That second part is true with butter, too.) And while you won't get that sweet mouthful of moo-fat, you will have a surprisingly moist and tender grouse none the less.

COOKING

1. Preheat the oven to 350°F. In a small bowl, combine the olive oil, sage leaves, salt, and pepper. Stir to combine.
2. Check the grouse: Trim any rough edges, pull any leftover feathers, rinse and rub out (with paper towels) any remnant of internal organs. Dry inside and out with paper towels.
3. Place a rack in a small baking dish, and place the bird on the rack. Rub the bird, especially the breast and legs, with the olive oil mixture. Place in the center of the oven.
4. Roast about 35 minutes, basting three times during cooking, and again when you take the bird out of the oven. A meat thermometer stuck in the thickest part of the thigh should register 150°F. Let the bird sit 10 minutes to allow the juices to saturate the meat; then carve and serve hot. Or chill and serve as a snack or a meal with pickled beets and sliced raw vegetables. ◉

Letting Birds Cool Before Carving

There's an old hunter's tale that if you let wild meat sit for 10 minutes before cutting into it, the meat will turn to mutton. That's not true. However, cutting into meat fresh from the oven will make it dry. Since this is mostly done with wild meat (because of all those old hunters) it supports that other age-old legend: Game is dry.

One of the easiest ways to refute both myths is to let the bird sit 10 minutes (after you've cooked them to a maximum of 150°F). During cooking, the animal's natural juices zap around under the skin like a miniature Pony Express. If you don't give those lovely juices time to settle back down into the meat, they will just roll off onto the cutting board. Or your kitchen counter. I'd rather have them basting the meat, wouldn't you? So let your birds (all your wild meat for that matter) sit 10 minutes before carving. They'll be juicier, and they still won't taste like mutton.

Shot Shell Soup

serves 4

Ingredients

3 cups boiling water
3 teaspoons chicken soup base
1 cup frozen corn
2 cups diced leftover roasted meats
1 cup fresh salsa
½ teaspoon salt
¼ cup couscous

A variation on my favorite old fable—stone soup. It starts with a pot of boiling water. Add some of this and some of that—kind of the shotgun school of cooking. Any roast grouse left over in the fridge? It will work well in this soup. If you make your own stock, use that instead of commercial soup base.

COOKING

1. To the boiling water, add the chicken soup base, corn, meat, salsa, and salt.
2. When it comes back to a boil, add the couscous, cover the pot, and reduce the heat to a simmer.
3. Simmer about 5 minutes, until the couscous are obvious. Serve immediately, with hard rolls. ❀

Tips

Couscous is just another form of pasta. What makes it perfect for this dish? It's so small it cooks in 5 minutes. If you can't get couscous, use about ½ cup of leftover cooked rice.

Soup base is a low-salt variation on bouillon that's found in the soup section of the grocery store. I like the taste better for simple dishes like this, and it dissolves so easily, it can be added directly to the pot to power up flavor without excessive stirring.

America's Team Baked Ruffed Grouse

serves 6–10

Ingredients

2 16-ounce cans whole berry cranberry sauce
2 bottles (8 ounces each) Catalina dressing
2 pouches Lipton onion soup mix
8–9 whole ruffed grouse, plucked or skinned
2 ounces unsalted pecans, chopped

All over the country, this is the recipe that repeats itself more often than any other. Sure every region makes its mark on the recipe (in this case, it's the pecans), but the reason it's popular and adapted all over the country is that it's easy, basic, quick, and beyond delicious. Plus, it's a beautifully festive dish. By the way, has anyone ever seen someone use Lipton onion soup mix for soup?

COOKING

1. Preheat the oven to 350°F. In a covered roasting pan just large enough for all the birds to fit cheek to cheek, mix together the cranberry sauce, dressing, and soup mix. (Heat the cranberry sauce a bit to liquefy it, if you want.)
2. Place the grouse breasts in the roasting pan, breast side up, and ladle the sauce over them. Cover and place in the center of the oven. Roast about 40 minutes, basting three or four times during the cooking.
3. Remove the grouse from the roaster and arrange on a heated serving platter. Pour the sauce over the grouse, and sprinkle with the chopped pecans. Serve immediately over rice. ❋

Tangy Creamed Ruffed Grouse with Roasted Vegetables

serves 4

Ingredients

FOR THE VEGGIES

1 tablespoon oil
¼ teaspoon salt
¼ teaspoon pepper
1 tablespoon dry onion flakes
4 medium potatoes, quartered
4 medium carrots, halved

FOR THE GROUSE

2 tablespoons Dijon mustard
Juice of 1 lemon, about 6 tablespoons
1 tablespoon honey, liquefied
¼ teaspoon sweet paprika
½ teaspoon dry mustard
½ cup cream
2 ruffed grouse, split
2 tablespoons butter

If you're looking for the classic creamed wild bird dish, this ain't it. If you're looking for a dish to wake up your senses—and fool your favorite nonhunter—this is the one. Use ruffed grouse, or any other pale-meated bird, including the naive fool's grouse (Franklin grouse) and the not-so-pale pheasant. Just be sure to turn the bird's leg-down in the sauce to ensure tender legs as well as juicy breasts.

COOKING

1. Preheat the oven to 350°F. In a small cup, combine the oil, salt, pepper, and onion flakes. Place the pieced potatoes and carrots in a plastic bag. Pour the seasoned oil over the vegetables, close the bag, and shake to coat completely.
2. Arrange the vegetables in a single layer in an 8-inch-square baking pan. Place in the center of the oven, and bake about 20 minutes by themselves. (They'll be joined soon by the birds and will take about 60 minutes all together.)
3. While the vegetables start roasting, begin the grouse. In a medium-sized bowl, combine the Dijon mustard, lemon juice, honey, paprika, and dry mustard. Measure out the cream but don't add it yet.

4. In a cast-iron skillet, just large enough for the four bird halves to lie flat in the bottom, gently brown the birds in the butter until both sides are just lightly browned. Finish with the birds skin-side down. Pour the cream into the mustard mixture and stir. Pour all of the sauce over and around the birds. Carefully nestle the birds down in the sauce so the legs are well covered.

5. Transfer the skillet to the oven, and roast 40 minutes with the vegetables. Serve bubbling hot, arranging a split half on each plate with the roasted vegetables, and sauce over both. ✽

Will's Blues

serves 2–4

Ingredients

1 can cream of celery soup
½ cup milk
1 teaspoon garlic powder
¼ teaspoon black pepper
2 grouse, whole with skin on or off

As his wife explains, Will is proud to be a Campbell's soup cook. And this is his favorite recipe. The funny thing is that it works with about any pale-meated bird you use. If your bird is a tough old veteran, Will suggests you parboil it first, for 60 minutes, with 1 tablespoon of pickling spices and just enough water to cover the birds. Drain the birds and proceed as usual.

COOKING

1. Preheat the oven to 350°F. In a baking dish just large enough for the grouse, combine the soup, milk, garlic powder, and pepper. Stir well.
2. Arrange the grouse, breast side up, and spoon the soup mixture over the top. Cover the roaster and place in the center of the oven. Roast about 60 minutes, basting often, until the meat falls off the bones. Serve with mashed potatoes, the pan gravy, and peas. ❀

Tarragon Blue Grouse

serves 2–4

Ingredients

1 blue grouse, whole
1 clove garlic, split
1 teaspoon fresh-minced tarragon
1 cup dry white wine

Josh is an avid hunter and takes a totally different approach to cooking grouse than her husband, Will, the Campbell's soup cook. This is her favorite birthday dish; guess who gets to cook it for her.

COOKING

1. Preheat oven to 325°F. Arrange the grouse in a small roaster pan, breast side up. Rub the outside of the grouse with the garlic; then discard the garlic. Sprinkle with the tarragon and pour the white wine into the bottom of the roaster pan.

2. Cook about one hour, until a meat thermometer registers about 150°F, basting with the white wine once or twice. Serve with buttered carrots and mashed potatoes. ✺

Mountain Lunch

makes 2 sandwiches

Ingredients

*1 whole ruffed or Franklin grouse (or ½ of a blue grouse),
    roasted and chilled*
½ cup lettuce
1 tomato sliced
2 teaspoons mayonnaise
Salt and pepper to taste
4 slices bread

Have any leftover mountain grouse in the fridge? Well, next time maybe you should cook two, because roast grouse—as well as pheasant, chukar, quail, and even Hungarian partridge—slice up into tasty sandwiches to eat at home or carry in the field on your next bird hunt.

PREPARATION

1. Slice the meat off the bones, including the thighs and drumsticks. Pull any remaining meat off the bones, including around and under the wishbone and the "oyster," a chunk of meat on the shoulder blade. (The bigger the bird, the bigger the oyster. Always look for it.)
2. Assemble the sandwiches: Lettuce and sliced tomato, followed by slices of meat, with enough mayonnaise to keep your whistle wet. (If it's a hot day and you are packing a lunch for the field, keep your lunch on ice or, if you're going to carry the sandwich in your vest, substitute mustard for the mayonnaise to prevent spoilage.) Season to taste with salt and pepper. ◉

Pocket Grouse

serves 2–4

Ingredients

2 grouse, whole with skin
2 tablespoons butter, melted
½ teaspoon salt
½ apple, cored and peeled
1 cup apple cider

Here's a recipe you can use in hunting camp or in your home kitchen without getting any pans dirty. Use paper plates, and the whole meal is mess-free—and incredibly simple. It works well with both small and large grouse. So use any blue, ruffed, or spruce that comes to hand.

COOKING

1. Preheat the oven to 375°F. Center a length of heavy-duty foil on a baking pan or cookie sheet. The foil should be long enough to wrap both grouse in the same package. Place the grouse in the middle. Brush both with the melted butter and sprinkle with salt. Insert ¼ of an apple inside each bird. Fold the foil up around the birds and pour the cider into the pocket. Close the foil.
2. Roast the bird for 45 minutes closed up. Open the foil and cook an additional 15 minutes to brown the breasts.
3. Serve with cornbread and Pocket Veggies (below). ❀

Pocket Veggies

Combine 1 cup corn, 1 cup sliced carrots, and 1 cup diced potatoes in a foil packet. Season with ½ teaspoon salt, ¼ teaspoon pepper, and dot liberally with butter. Seal and toss into the oven with the grouse. The vegetables will be ready when the grouse is done.

Creamy Ginger Grouse

serves 4

Ingredients

⅓ cup diced green onion
2 tablespoons butter or margarine
1½ cups thinly sliced carrots
½ cup dry white wine
1 tablespoon freshly grated ginger
¾ cup heavy cream
¼ teaspoon black pepper (or lemon pepper)
1 pound diced grouse breast (ruffed, blue, or spruce),
    2½–3 cups
4 slices toast or 3 cups cooked rice

Here's a quick dish that will win the hearts of your family. It's so quick that you'll want to have everything cut, diced, and measured before you heat up the frying pan. And have the rice or toast ready, too.

COOKING

1. In a large skillet, sauté the onions in the butter; add the carrots and cook until just tender, about 2 minutes. Stir in the wine and grated ginger. When the wine comes to a low simmer, add the cream, salt, and pepper.

2. Bring the sauce back to a low simmer and cook slowly, stirring often, until the sauce thickens. (It should be the consistency of turkey gravy.)

3. Add the diced grouse meat to the pan and cook 2 minutes, stirring the meat into the sauce so it is covered completely.

4. Serve over rice or, for a truly easy Saturday night dinner, a slice of toast. ◉

Tip

This dish deserves freshly grated ginger. To get 1 tablespoon, buy at least 3 inches of ginger-root. Pick a plump, heavy, firm root; avoid anything that looks shriveled or dried. To grate, cut away the pulpy outer skin and grate on the medium hole of your grater—as you would carrots for a salad.

Royal Blues in Creamy Balsamic Vinegar Sauce

serves 2

Ingredients

16 ounces very good balsamic vinegar
3 tablespoons butter, in all
1 cup cream
Breast meat of 1 ruffed or Franklin grouse, (or ½ blue),
  sliced across the grain
Pinch of fresh basil, minced
Pinch of fresh oregano, minced
1 tablespoon ripe tomato, minced and seeded
4 cups cooked ziti or rotini pasta

It's a joy to occasionally discover a restaurant and a cook with a great idea for game. Aunt Sophie's Restaurant in Bozeman, Montana, is just such a place; Dan Bridges, born and raised in Bozeman, is just such a cook. This sauce is a bit time consuming, but the reduction can be done ahead of time and creates enough balsamic syrup to practice the dish before you go out and impress your friends. And you *will* want to cook this unique sauce for your friends.

 Don't worry if you don't have a blue grouse; any tender, pale-fleshed bird will do.

PREPARATION

1. Days ahead of time, so it doesn't even seem to be connected, pour the whole bottle of balsamic vinegar in a good-quality heavy-bottomed saucepan.
2. Bring the vinegar to a simmer and let it simmer at the back of the stove until reduced to about one fourth (about ½ cup of vinegar). Remove pan from the heat and set it aside. When cool, place it in a glass bottle with a cap that can be sealed tightly. The reduced vinegar will taste slightly sweet, completely unlike vinegar. Store in the refrigerator until ready to use.

COOKING

1. Melt 1 tablespoon of the butter in a small heavy-bottomed saucepan or frying pan over medium-low heat. (I use an enamel-coated cast-iron omelet pan with curved sides for easier stirring.) Once the butter is liquefied, pour in the cream and 2 level teaspoons of the reduced balsamic vinegar. Stir to combine.
2. Bring the cream to a simmer over medium-low heat, then continue simmering, stirring constantly with a whisk or rubber spatula until the cream is reduced by about half. Put some music on, this sauce is going to take 20-30 minutes to reduce depending on how brave you are, and it will take your undivided attention. When

done, the sauce will be thick enough to coat a spoon, and it will have the color and consistency of milk chocolate pudding. Turn off the heat.

3. In a second skillet, melt another tablespoon of butter over medium-high heat. When the butter starts to sizzle, add the sliced breast meat and quickly sauté, for about 3 to 4 minutes, until lightly browned. Cover to keep warm.

4. Finish the sauce: Bring the sauce back up to a simmer, add the last tablespoon of butter, and whisk the sauce until the butter is completely melted and the sauce is starting to bubble lightly again. Toss the sautéed breast meat in the cream sauce; add the basil, oregano, and tomato. Stir and pour over the pasta. Serve immediately, with a toast to Dan Bridges and Aunt Sophie's Restaurant. ⊛

Chapter Two

Quail

Quail Bobs with Peanut Sauce

serves 4 as a main course

Ingredients

FOR THE BIRDS
12 10-inch wooden skewers
Boned breasts of 12 quail

FOR THE PEANUT SAUCE
2 tablespoons creamy peanut butter
2 tablespoons freshly squeezed lime juice (1 lime)
2 tablespoons soy sauce
1 tablespoon plus 1 teaspoon honey
½ teaspoon curry powder
½ teaspoon red pepper flakes
¼ teaspoon lime zest
2 tablespoons oil

Use these bobs as an appetizer or for the main course. But allow at least 2–3 birds for each person if that's all the protein they're eating. That will give you about 4 ounces of meat for each person.

COOKING

1. Cover the wooden skewers with cold water and let soak 30 minutes. Check breasts for shot, bone chips, and rough edges. Slice each half-breast in half lengthwise. In a small blender, combine the peanut butter, lime juice, soy sauce, honey, curry powder, red pepper flakes, and lime zest. Purée and set aside.

2. Preheat the barbecue to medium-high heat. Thread the breast slices on the wooden skewers, brush with oil.

3. When the barbecue is ready, place the skewers on the cooking grate directly over the fire. Turn every 2–3 minutes, cooking about 10 minutes in all. Brush generously with the peanut sauce and serve immediately. ✹

What the Heck is Zest?

Zest refers to the very thin green surface over the lime. It's full of oil and incredible flavor—much more flavor than just the juice. The trick is to remove the outer layer (the green layer for limes, yellow layer for lemons, orange for oranges) without getting any of the bitter white rind underneath.

You can buy a "zester." It looks like a miniature garden rake with circles instead of tines at the business end that scrape just to the right depth. Or use a light touch with a potato peeler or a fine cheese grater.

Spicy Buffalo Breasts

serves 4

Ingredients

6 ounces unsweetened pineapple juice
3 tablespoons Louisiana hot sauce
2 tablespoons sour cream
1 teaspoon paprika
1 teaspoon sugar
Breasts of 10–12 quail with breastbones attached
2 tablespoons butter

For those who like the spicy food, and even for those who don't, here's a variation on the hot wings so popular as restaurant appetizers. We're using breasts because wild bird wings don't have enough meat on their wings to bother with. You can cook these breasts two ways: with the breastbone still attached (as described here), or boned, put on kabobs, and cooked about 5 minutes on a hot grill. (If you grill, however, add 1 teaspoon of cornstarch to the marinade while still cold. Bring it to a boil in a small saucepan and simmer it 4 minutes, but do time this before you dip cooked birds in it. The simmering kills any bugs the raw meat left behind.

PREPARATION

1. In a resealable plastic bag, combine the pineapple juice, hot sauce, sour cream, paprika, and sugar. Close the bag and shake to mix the marinade.
2. Rinse the birds and trim away any rough edges. Dry with paper towels and place in the marinade. Let the birds marinate in the refrigerator 8–24 hours.

COOKING

1. Remove the birds from the marinade and save the marinade. Shake off excess liquid from the birds.
2. Melt the butter in a small skillet and gently brown the breasts until just lightly golden.
3. Add the marinade to the skillet, and bring to a boil. Lower the heat to the lowest setting and simmer, covered, for 15 minutes. Serve hot with cold beer.

Tip

Louisiana hot sauces vary by brand. Choose a moderate hot sauce—not one of the ultra-hot brands—and add it one tablespoon at a time, tasting as you go. Three tablespoons of my hot sauce gives this a good bite without making my mouth burn for 20 minutes afterwards.

Beer Batter Bites

serves 4

Ingredients

1½ cups flour
1 teaspoon dried leaf basil
1 teaspoon dried leaf oregano
1 teaspoon salt
½ teaspoon pepper
2 egg yolks, beaten
1 cup beer
Boned breasts of 20 quail

For those who bone out their quail, there may be nothing more sumptuous than these fried morsels. No dip required.

PREPARATION

In a medium-sized bowl, combine the flour, basil, oregano, salt, pepper, and egg yolks. Mix to combine, then add the beer, stirring well. Cover and place in the refrigerator 2–3 hours.

COOKING

1. Preheat a deep fryer to 350°–375°F. In the meantime, set the breast meat out in a double layer of paper towels to absorb excess moisture.
2. Dip the breasts in the beer batter and gently drop into the hot oil. Fry until golden brown. Drain on paper towels a few minutes, and enjoy. ⊛

A Braised Brace of Quail

serves 2

Ingredients

⅓ cup red wine vinegar
⅓ cup brown sugar
4 quail, halved
1 tablespoon oil
1 sweet yellow bell pepper, sliced thin

I like the elegance of serving this dish with quail that have been split up the middle (see page 161 for instructions). But there's a practical element, too. Wingshot quail, more than other birds, often have a good and a bad side. Use the good side of the bird for this dish, then pick through the bad side for empanadas or kabobs (recipes elsewhere in this chapter). If all you have in the freezer is boned breasts, they'll work, too. Just try to use the younger, more tender birds, since this dish doesn't cook very long. By the way, yellow bell peppers are just a riper version of the more common green peppers. The ripeness goes from green to red to orange to yellow. The riper the pepper, the milder the flavor. Either orange or yellow will work here.

COOKING

1. Combine the vinegar and brown sugar in a bowl. Split the quail and wipe them inside and out with paper towels. Remove any loose bones and trim rough edges.
2. In a 10-inch skillet, heat the oil over medium-high heat, then sear the skin side of the quail until lightly golden brown, about 2–3 minutes. Turn the quail skin side up, toss the peppers across the top of them, and pour the sweetened vinegar over everything.
3. Cover the pan and reduce the heat to low. Continue cooking for approximately 10 minutes more, until the quail are done. Serve over rice. ◉

Citrus Quail

serves 4

Ingredients

Juice of 1 orange (about ¾ cup)
Juice of 1 lemon (about ¼ cup)
8 whole quail, cleaned and plucked
½ cup flour
½ teaspoon salt
¼ teaspoon pepper
5 tablespoons butter
1 teaspoon chicken bouillon granules
½ cup hot water
1 orange, quartered and sliced thick with peel on

For the larger, older, and tougher quail in your game vest, you need a recipe that gives these delicious birds a chance to grow more tender. This is a tart and tangy recipe, but if you prefer sweeter sauces, add 1–2 table-spoons of brown sugar to the chicken bouillon. If all you have in the freezer is tender young birds, they'll work, too.

PREPARATION

Combine the orange and lemon juice in a resealable plastic bag. Rinse and dry the quail. Place the birds in the marinade and let sit overnight in the refrigerator.

COOKING

1. In a small plastic bag, combine the flour, salt, and pepper. Shake the marinade off the birds, and toss them in the flour, 2 at a time. Shake off the excess flour. In a 10-inch covered skillet or saucepan, melt the butter until it just starts to sizzle over medium heat. Lightly sauté the quail in the butter until they are golden, about 4–5 minutes.

2. Dissolve the chicken bouillon in the hot water and add it to the pan. Pour in the marinade as well. When the pan comes back up to a simmer, add the orange slices, cover, and reduce the heat to low. Simmer about 30 minutes or until the quail are tender, basting the birds about every 10 minutes. The sauce will thicken on its own as it cooks. Serve with sliced carrots cooked with a dab of butter. ✺

Quail Empanadas

Ingredients

FOR THE EMPANADAS
2 cups shredded cooked quail meat
1 cup fresh tomato salsa
12 sheets egg roll wrappers
1 egg white

FOR THE DIP
½ cup sour cream
¾ teaspoon ground cumin
¼ teaspoon chili powder
½ teaspoon onion powder
½ teaspoon green pepper Tabasco sauce
¼ teaspoon salt

Empanadas, meat-filled turnovers from south of the border, are great deep-fried and then dipped in a tasty sour cream sauce. They can be a meal in themselves or a party appetizer. Don't be afraid to substitute any white-meated bird for the quail. Leftovers never tasted so good.

COOKING

1. In a small bowl, combine the shredded quail meat and the salsa. Stir and set aside. In a second small bowl, combine the dip ingredients. Set that aside, too. Now preheat your deep-fat fryer to 350°–375°F. (A Fry Daddy works well.)

2. Lay out the egg roll wrappers on a cutting board. Cut each in half and in half again so that you have four 3-inch squares. Lay a teaspoon of the salsa mixture into the middle of each square, wipe the edges with egg white, and fold the wrapper over to seal. Once you get a few made, you can start frying the empanadas 2 or 3 at a time. Fry until golden brown, about 3–4 minutes each. Serve with dip. ⊛

Tips

For a low-fat alternative, place the empanadas on a lightly oiled baking sheet and place in a 400°F oven for 8 minutes, turning once. Serve with additional fresh salsa instead of the sour cream dip.

If you don't have leftover quail meat, slice up about 6 ounces (1 cup) of quail breast, then lightly sauté in 2 teaspoons of olive oil for 4–5 minutes. Stir as the meat sautés and add ¼ teaspoon salt and ⅛ teaspoon black pepper as it finishes. Turn the sautéed meat out onto paper towels, cool, and chop. Continue as above.

Quail Cacciatore

serves 2

Ingredients

2 strips bacon
1 tablespoon olive oil
1 medium onion, chopped
3 cloves garlic, minced
1 teaspoon dried leaf sage
½ teaspoon dried rosemary, crushed
½ teaspoon black pepper
½ cup dry white wine (not aged in oak)
1 14.5-ounce can peeled whole tomatoes
8 ounces sliced quail breast (1⅓ cups)
½ teaspoon salt
2 tablespoons fresh minced parsley
1 teaspoon lemon zest

In Italian, cacciatore is the hunter—so this is truly the hunter's dish. Make it with your favorite pale-to-medium-meated bird; in addition to quail you can use Hungarian and chukar partridge, pheasant, and the light-meated mountain grouse. Don't forget the lemon zest and parsley at the end. It is the powder in this cacciatore's charge.

COOKING

1. In a large skillet, lightly brown the bacon in the oil over medium heat. Add the onion, garlic, sage, rosemary, and pepper and continue sautéing until the onions begin to color, about 8–10 minutes.
2. Raise the heat to high and add the white wine to the skillet. Continue cooking the wine until the pan is almost dry, about 3–4 minutes.
3. Reduce the heat to medium and add the tomatoes and sliced quail meat. Stir to coat the meat. Once the skillet comes to a low simmer, reduce the heat to low and cover the pan with the lid tipped slightly to allow steam to escape. Simmer about 10–15 minutes, allowing the meat and tomatoes to swap flavors with the bacon and herbs.
4. Just before serving, add the salt. (Taste first. Your white wine might be saltier than mine.) Then add the parsley and lemon zest. Serve over pasta. ✵

Cashew Quail

serves 4

Ingredients

2 teaspoons cornstarch
2 teaspoons dry sherry
½ teaspoon grated fresh ginger
8 ounces (1⅓ cups) diced quail meat
3 tablespoons soy sauce
3 tablespoons hoisin sauce
1 tablespoon sugar
3 tablespoons water
2 tablespoons canola or peanut oil
¾ cup whole, unsalted cashews
3 cups cooked rice

The hoisin sauce in this recipe is a common ingredient in Chinese cooking. It adds a tangy, solid flavor to this dish. Look for it in the "Asian" food section of your grocery store. And if you can't find completely unsalted cashews, use the least salty ones available.

COOKING

1. In a small bowl combine the cornstarch, sherry, and ginger. Stir well. Add the diced quail, toss to coat the meat completely and set the bowl aside. In a second small bowl, combine the soy sauce, hoisin sauce, sugar, and water. Stir and set aside.
2. Heat the oil in a large skillet or wok over high heat until wisps of smoke just start to come off the oil. Add the cashews and the diced quail (with ginger marinade) to the hot oil and let that cook, stirring constantly until the cashews start to brown, no more than 3–4 minutes.

Why Canola Oil ?

Wok cooking is best when done at high heat, and many cooking oils will burn before reaching optimal temperature. That burnt flavor latches onto your dinner. So when frying at high temperatures, you need oil with a high smoking point, and the highest is peanut oil. As far as your health is concerned, you should be using oil with the most omega-3 fatty acids—like olive oil. The compromise is canola oil. It has almost as much good fat as olive oil, and almost as high a smoking point as peanut oil. Plus, it costs less than either one.

3. Add the soy sauce mixture to the pan and toss the quail and cashews into the sauce. Continue cooking over high heat until the sauce thickens, about 1 minute. Serve immediately over rice. ◉

Making Rice

Bring 1½ cups of water to a boil in a small covered saucepan. Stir in 1 cup of raw rice. Cover the pot, lower the heat to simmer, and set a timer for 15 minutes. The rice is done when it forms "eyes"—holes in the surface of the rice—and has no liquid in the bottom of the pot when you stir it up. This will yield about 3 cups cooked rice.

Creamy Mary Quail

serves 4

Ingredients

1 12-ounce can 2% evaporated milk
1 cup bottled Bloody Mary mix
1 tablespoon jalapeño peppers
1 large egg
1 teaspoon salt
¼ teaspoon red pepper Tabasco sauce
3 tablespoons oil, in all
2 cups chopped onion
4 cups frozen hash browns, thawed
1 pound boned meat, breast or thighs, cubed (3 cups)
1 cup grated Cheddar cheese

Some dishes are light and fresh—just made for a hot summer night. Not this Creamy Mary. She's a rich, stick-to-your-ribs dish that not only warms up the kitchen but also comforts your frozen limbs on a cold winter's night.

COOKING

1. In a large bowl, combine the evaporated milk and the Bloody Mary mix. Pour about ¼ cup of this mixture into a processor and add the jalapeño pepper and egg. Process on high for a few seconds until it all turns to a liquid—especially the jalapeños. Return this mixture to the large bowl and add the salt and Tabasco sauce. Set aside. Preheat the oven to 300°F.

2. In a 3-quart Dutch oven, heat the oil over medium-high heat and sauté the onions and hashed browns together until both begin to brown, about 4–5 minutes if the potatoes were at room temperature.

3. Pour in the evaporated milk mixture and stir the hash browns into the sauce. Bring the sauce to a low simmer, add the meat, cover, and transfer to the hot oven.

4. Bake 30 minutes covered. Remove the cover and bake another 10 minutes to brown the top. Remove the dish from the oven, sprinkle the cheese across the top, and cover the dish. Let it sit 5 minutes while the cheese melts. Serve hot. ✹

White-On-White Chili

serves 6

Ingredients

FOR SOAKING THE BEANS
1 cup white navy beans
3 cups water

FOR COOKING THE BEANS
4 cups water
4 teaspoons chicken bouillon granules
½ medium yellow onion, chopped
1 clove garlic, minced

TO ASSEMBLE THE CHILI
2 tablespoons oil
1 clove garlic, minced
½ yellow onion, chopped
1 teaspoon dried leaf oregano
½ teaspoon ground cumin
½ teaspoon salt
¼ teaspoon chili powder
¼ teaspoon cayenne pepper
2 pounds quail meat, diced (5–6 cups)
2 whole canned chili peppers, diced
¼ cup cream
½ cup grated Monterey Jack cheese

One of the great things about going to the Helena, Montana, gun show is the endless crock of white chili O'Brien's has simmering away at the snack bar. This pot isn't endless, but it's a delicious variation on that classic favorite.

PREPARATION

1. Start at least the day before, or as many as 5 or 6 days ahead. Soak the beans in the water overnight. Drain the

beans, rinse well, and transfer to a large pot.

2. Add the water, bouillon granules, yellow onion, and garlic to the beans. Bring to a boil, reduce the heat to a simmer, and cover the pot. Let the beans cook for 2 hours, until they are tender. Set aside until you are ready to assemble the chili.

ASSEMBLING THE CHILI

1. In a 3-quart Dutch oven, heat the oil over medium heat and sauté the garlic and onions until tender. Add the oregano, cumin, salt, chili powder, and cayenne pepper. Stir well.

2. When you begin to smell the spices, add the diced quail meat and sauté until the meat is opaque. Add the chili peppers and cooked beans (with cooking liquid) and bring the saucepan back up to a simmer. Add the cream and cook until the chili is hot again.

3. Serve hot in soup bowls with a generous sprinkle of cheese on top. ❀

Chapter Three

Pheasants

Grilled Pheasant Breast with Fresh Apricot-Kumquat Salsa

serves 2

Ingredients

FOR THE MARINADE

Juice of 1 freshly squeezed medium orange (about ½ cup)
Juice of 1 freshly squeezed medium lime (about ¼ cup)
¼ small white onion
1 clove garlic
1 raw serrano chili (3 inches long)
½ teaspoon salt
¼ teaspoon pepper
Boned breast of one pheasant

FOR THE SALSA

2 kumquats
1 apricot, pitted and diced
2 teaspoons minced fresh cilantro
2 teaspoons minced white onion
¼ teaspoon salt

FOR THE COOKING

Oil
Mesquite chips

Kumquat. This odd-sounding fruit may be unfamiliar, but if you just try one, you'll be hooked. The flavor? It's a cross between a tangerine and a tree-ripened Arizona orange: very sweet, fresh, and tangy. Perfect for this salsa, especially since kumquats appear in the grocery store in the heart of grilling season. If you can't find kumquats, use the zest of a tangerine, with a teaspoon of its freshly squeezed juice.

PREPARATION

1. For the marinade: In a blender, combine the orange juice, lime juice, onion, garlic, and serrano chili. Purée until smooth. Pour into a resealable plastic bag and add the salt, pepper, and pheasant breast. Refrigerate overnight.

2. Remove the seeds and pulp and place in a small bowl. Squeeze as much juice as possible from the pulp into a small bowl and discard the leftover pulp and seed. Dice the rind and add to the juice, along with the apricot, cilantro, and onion. Toss, cover, and refrigerate overnight. Add the salt just before you start cooking.

COOKING

1. Preheat the barbecue grill to medium-high heat. Drain the marinade and discard.

2. Lightly oil the pheasant breast and grill about 3–4 minutes a side until the pink is just gone. Serve immediately with the apricot-kumquat salsa. Serve grilled red and green bell peppers, onions, and corn on the cob as side dishes, and flan for dessert. ⊛

Using Serrano Chilies

Here's a classic case of not being able to judge a book by its cover. Serrano chilies look a lot like jalapeño peppers. But the taste is surprising: a cross between a sweet bell pepper and its look-alike cousin. Use rubber gloves when handling all peppers. If you live closer to the Mexican border than my Helena, Montana, Safeway, be warned: chilies are hotter the closer they are to the Mexican border. This recipe is for Montana serrano chilies, which are simply not as strong.

Grilled Splits with Spicy Orange Glaze

serves 2–4

Ingredients

¼ cup orange marmalade, liquified
1 teaspoon green pepper Tabasco sauce
Split breasts of 2 pheasants

Summer dinner is a snap with an easy-to-mix bar-becue sauce and large, juicy, delicious pheasant breasts. Use a young bird and follow the directions on pages 169–170 for removing the sternum. Your family won't believe those big juicy slices of meat you're serving come from a little wild bird. And if you've already boned out that bird, allow about one half the cooking time.

COOKING

1. Preheat your barbecue to about 400°F, or medium to medium-hot. In a small bowl, combine the orange marmalade and the green pepper sauce. Stir to combine.
2. Lay both split breasts on a cutting board, skin side up. Spread the marmalade-pepper mixture across them.
3. Rub a bit of oil on the back of each breast. Place on the grill. Close the grill cover and cook about 8 minutes skin side up. Turn to sear the skin, about 3–4 minutes. The breasts are done when you prick the side with a paring knife and the juices run clear or slightly pink.
4. To serve, cut both breasts across the grain, leaving the wing bones in. Serve hot with potato and 3-bean salad.⊛

Deep-Fried Lemon-Pepper Pheasant

serves 4

Ingredients

½ cup freshly squeezed lemon juice
¼ cup softened butter
1½ teaspoons black pepper
1 teaspoon onion powder
¼ teaspoon garlic salt
½ teaspoon dry lemon peel (granulated, in jars)
1 teaspoon sugar
1 teaspoon salt
2 teaspoons lemon zest
2 whole pheasants, plucked
Oil for frying

Everybody deep-fries turkeys. But pheasants are just as moist and delicious as turkeys when prepared this way, maybe more so. And they take only 7 minutes if you're at 375° to 400°F; 8 minutes if you're at 350°F.

COOKING

1. In a small bowl, combine the lemon juice, butter, pepper, onion powder, garlic salt, lemon peel, sugar, salt, and zest. Load this marinade into an injector syringe and inject about half the mixture into the breasts and half into the legs of both birds. Let them marinate while you heat the oil.

2. Preheat about 4–5 gallons of oil to 350°F in a turkey fryer. When the oil is hot, place one pheasant on the cooking rack and slowly plunge it into the oil. Cook 7 to 8 minutes.

3. Remove the first bird and let it drip over paper towels several minutes before you remove it from the rack. Use thick oven mitts to do this, as the pheasant will still be hot. Place the cooked bird breast up on paper towels (or a metal cooling rack if you have one, with towels beneath.) Arrange the second pheasant on the rack, and cook it 7 to 8 minutes. Remove from the oil, and let the second bird cool on the rack until you can handle it, about 15 minutes.

4. Carve the birds as you would a Christmas turkey. Slice through the skin between the thigh and breast and remove the legs at the hip joint. Then slice the breast meat from the bone, or cut the breast off whole and slice across the grain. Serve hot or cold with pasta salad.

Tip

If you want to deep-fry skinned birds, dip them in a tempura batter before you cook them. The tempura will seal the juices into the meat almost as effectively as the skin does. For a simple tempura: Combine 1½ cups flour; 1 teaspoon each of dried leaf basil, dried leaf oregano, and salt; ½ teaspoon pepper; 2 beaten yolks; and about ⅞ cup of beer. Beat 2 egg whites until stiff but not dry and fold that in. Dip the birds. The batter won't be especially pretty but it will save the pheasant's skin, so to speak.

Rooster Wraps

makes 4 sandwiches

Ingredients

4 cups leftover pheasant meat, dark or white
1 tablespoon Dijon mustard
1 tablespoon mayonnaise
4 flour tortillas, 8-inch diameter
Lettuce
Sliced tomato
Sliced cucumber
Dill pickles

PREPARATION

1. Slice the meat thin from a previously cooked pheasant. This is a good way to use meat from all around the carcass—check for small chunks of meat under and around the wishbone and don't forget the oyster sitting on the shoulder blade on the upper back.

2. Combine the mustard and mayonnaise. Lay the tortillas on a cutting board and spread each with the mayonnaise mixture. Arrange some lettuce, tomato, cucumber, and ¼ of the meat in the middle of each tortilla. Then fold the bottom of the tortilla up and the two sides over the filling. Serve with dill pickles and chips for a summer lunch. ✸

Teriyaki Kabobs with Wasabi Dip

serves 4

Ingredients

FOR THE MARINADE

¼ cup oil
⅜ cup lite soy sauce
2 tablespoons brown sugar
¼ teaspoon garlic powder
1 tablespoon medium-dry sherry
¾ teaspoon ground ginger

FOR COOKING

Breast of one pheasant, cut in ¾-inch strips
4 wooden skewers
1 tablespoon cornstarch
4 teaspoons wasabi powder
3 teaspoons cold water

Teriyaki is a very effective tenderizing marinade when you want to quick-cook meats. The wasabi, Japanese horseradish, is a bonus. It's sold in both powder and paste forms. The paste is ready to use; the powder must be mixed with water and is traditionally rolled into a ball for serving. You may need to adjust the water-to-powder ratio, but if you can roll it into a ball easily, it's ready to eat. (As with chilies, wash hands carefully after handling wasabi.)

PREPARATION

1. The night before: In a sealable bag, combine the oil, soy sauce, brown sugar, garlic powder, sherry, and ginger. Rinse and dry the boned pheasant breast and add to the marinade bag. Shake to coat the meat. Marinate in the refrigerator for 24 hours.
2. Thirty minutes before cooking: Soak the wooden skewers in cold water for 30 minutes to keep them from burning on the grill.

COOKING

1. Preheat the grill to medium-high heat (about 450°–500°F at cooking level). Drain the marinade into a small saucepan. (You should have about ¾ cup of marinade.) Add the cornstarch and stir well. Once the cornstarch has dissolved, cook over medium heat, stirring constantly,

until the marinade comes to a boil and thickens. Remove from heat immediately and set aside.

2. Thread the pheasant strips onto the skewers and brush with the marinade. In a small bowl, combine the wasabi powder and water, stirring until it forms a paste. Roll the paste into a ball (adding powder or water as needed to roll easily).

3. Place the skewers on the grill. Cook about 3 minutes a side. Remove and serve with a small amount of wasabi. My favorite side dish with these skewers is grilled acorn squash. Slice the squash about ¼-inch thin, microwave until semi-soft (about 1½ minutes on high/700 watts). Then grill, brushing them with the marinade as well. ✿

Pheasant Poppers

serves 2–4

Ingredients

FOR ITALIAN
1 cup dry bread crumbs
3 tablespoons dry leaf basil
2 teaspoons dry leaf thyme
3 tablespoons dry onion flakes
4 teaspoons salt

FOR MEXICAN
1 cup bread crumbs
4 teaspoons ground cumin
1½ teaspoons garlic salt
2 tablespoons dry leaf oregano
1 teaspoon chili powder
1 teaspoon salt
½ teaspoon black pepper

FOR INDIAN CURRY
1 cup dry bread crumbs
4 teaspoons curry powder
2 teaspoons salt

FOR THE PHEASANT
8 ounces (1⅓ cups) boned pheasant breast, diced in bite-sized pieces
    (about 1 inch thick)
Peanut or canola oil
1 cup flour
1 egg, beaten
½ cup ranch dressing

Dipping fried food in ranch dressing is a popular custom where I live. While these poppers are juicy, tender, and delicious without any dip (or with a low-cal chili sauce or even ketchup), you should at least try them with creamy ranch. Heat addicts may want to add a few drops of Tabasco sauce to the egg, with the Mexican version. Each spice mix will coat 8 ounces of meat.

COOKING

1. Let the pheasant meat come to room temperature. Preheat a deep-fat fryer to 350°–375°F. In a small bowl, mix one (your choice) of the seasoned bread crumb mixes. Set it aside. Put the egg in a second bowl and the flour in a third.
2. Starting with the flour bowl, followed by the egg and the bread crumbs, dredge, dip, and dredge the pheasant bites. Fry in small batches until deep golden brown (about 2–3 minutes). Remove from the fryer and drain on paper towels.
3. Serve immediately as an appetizer or snack with creamy ranch dressing, chili sauce, or plain. ❀

Chinese Waldorf Salad

serves 4

Ingredients

FOR THE MARINADE

½ cup soy sauce
1 tablespoon minced crystallized ginger
1 tablespoon brown sugar
1 tablespoon rice wine vinegar
8- to 10-ounce pheasant breast, boned

FOR ASSEMBLING THE SALAD

1 cup chopped walnuts
1 cup chopped apple
1 cup chopped celery
⅔ cup mayonnaise

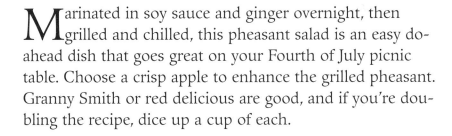

Marinated in soy sauce and ginger overnight, then grilled and chilled, this pheasant salad is an easy do-ahead dish that goes great on your Fourth of July picnic table. Choose a crisp apple to enhance the grilled pheasant. Granny Smith or red delicious are good, and if you're doubling the recipe, dice up a cup of each.

PREPARATION

1. Combine the soy sauce, ginger, sugar, and vinegar in a resealable plastic bag. Seal and shake well. Add the pheasant breast and shake again. Marinate overnight in the refrigerator.
2. Pour off the marinade and lightly rub the breast with oil. Preheat your grill to medium-high heat. Grill about 2 minutes a side. Chill 30–60 minutes.

TO ASSEMBLE THE SALAD

1. Dice the pheasant breast into ½-inch pieces.
2. In a large bowl, toss the pheasant pieces, walnuts, apple, and celery to mix. Fold the mayonnaise into the salad. Serve on toast or with sliced tomato and lettuce. ❈

Poached Pheasant Salad

serves 4

Ingredients

FOR POACHING

3 teaspoons chicken soup base
3 cups water
¾ cup mild tomato salsa
¾ teaspoon salt
¾ teaspoon green pepper Tabasco sauce
Breast of 1 pheasant, boned and skinned

FOR ASSEMBLING THE SALAD

⅔ cup diced cucumber (about ½ cucumber)
⅔ cup diced celery (1–2 stalks)
½ cup mayonnaise
10–20 drops red pepper Tabasco sauce

Here's one of our favorite chicken dishes turned on its head. I use mild salsa to poach the pheasant; if you like to heat things up, use hot salsa instead. But don't get intimidated by this 2-step recipe. Poaching is simply cooking at a very low boil, and once the liquid starts to bubble, just set a timer—it cooks by itself.

PREPARATION

1. In a small saucepan, combine the soup base, water, salsa, salt, and green Tabasco sauce. Stir well to combine. Place the pheasant breast in the saucepan.
2. Bring the saucepan just to a boil and immediately turn the heat down to low for a very gentle simmer. (No rolling boil, please. Poaching is a very gentle process. Poach for 60 minutes, uncovered, or until the meat is tender.
3. Remove the pheasant breast from the poaching liquid and chill overnight in a covered container.

ASSEMBLY

1. Chop the pheasant meat into ½-inch cubes and add to the diced cucumber and celery. Toss gently.
2. In a small bowl, combine the mayonnaise and Tabasco sauce. Gently toss with the rest of the ingredients until everything is coated with the mayonnaise. Serve on sliced tomato or in sandwiches. ❀

Tortilla Soup

serves 4

Ingredients

2 cloves garlic, minced
1 cup chopped onion
2 tablespoons olive oil
1 teaspoon ground cumin
1 teaspoon chili powder
8 ounces (1⅓ cups) pheasant breast meat, diced
¼ cup raw white rice
2 cans (14½ ounces each) low-sodium chicken broth
2 teaspoons canned green chilies, diced
4 corn tortillas
Oil for frying
2 tablespoons sour cream

I love soups that are quick but substantial enough to serve as an entire meal. If you have several birds in the freezer, you can expand the recipe to feed a crowd. Doubled, it will fill a 5-quart pot, and the flavor only improves when served the next day. Ah, if only all leftovers tasted this good.

COOKING

1. In a medium-sized skillet, sauté the garlic and onion in the oil over medium heat until just soft. Stir in the cumin and chili powder. Stir the spices well, toss the pheasant meat into the seasoned onions, and cook for about 2 minutes until the meat is just cooked through. Stir the rice into the skillet and sauté it until warm, about 1 minute.
2. Add the chicken broth and chili peppers, stirring the pan juices up from the bottom. Bring to a boil, reduce the heat to low, and cover the pot. Simmer about 30 minutes, until the rice is cooked and the pheasant is tender.
3. With a pair of scissors, cut the tortillas into strips. Heat the oil (about ½-inch deep) in a skillet over medium-high heat. Fry the tortilla strips a few at a time in the oil until they begin to brown. Drain on paper towels and let cool.
4. To assemble the soup: Place a few tortilla chips in the bottom of each soup bowl. Pour the soup over the tortilla chips, top each serving with a dollop of sour cream, and serve immediately. ⊛

Hot Ginger Pheasant Soup

serves 2–4

Ingredients

4 cups hot water
4 teaspoons chicken soup base
4 stalks lemon grass
2-inch cube of fresh ginger
1 diced serrano chili, seeded
¼ cup diced red bell pepper
8 ounces (1⅓ cups) diced pheasant breast meat
2 tablespoons heavy cream (optional)

Tip

Have you ever reached for a glass of water when you ate something too hot and found it did absolutely nothing to put out the fire? That's why there's cream in this recipe. Cream—actually anything dairy—is much more effective at curing the burn of chilies and other hot foods. That's probably why you see a lot of sour cream in Mexican dishes and cream in some Thai food. If you like hot foods, you can omit the cream. If, however, you're like me and have overactive taste buds, 1-2 tablespoons will be enough to let you taste the full range of flavors in this delicious soup without having to put up with the fire.

This recipe sounds a bit like a scavenger hunt. But relax. It's as versatile as you need it to be. If you don't have chicken soup base, for instance, use an equal amount of low-sodium chicken broth. If you can't get the lemon grass stalks, the zest (or yellow part of the rind) of half a lemon is a good substitute. And don't worry if you don't own a zester. It's a lot easier to just peel the lemon with a potato peeler, but use a light touch. All you want is the intensely flavored and microscopically thin yellow layer of the rind. That's where the rich lemony oils are. If you double or triple the recipe, be sure to double and triple everything, including the ginger and lemon grass.

COOKING

1. In a small saucepan, combine the water, soup base, lemon grass, and ginger. Bring to a rolling boil, and reduce to a simmer. Simmer, uncovered, for 15 minutes. Remove from heat, and when the pot is cool enough to handle, pour the broth through a strainer into a bowl. Toss the chunks of ginger and lemon grass and return the broth to the saucepan over medium-high heat.

2. Add the serrano chili, red bell pepper, and diced pheasant. When the soup comes back to a slow boil, reduce the heat to a simmer and cook about 15 minutes more. Add the cream just before serving. ◉

Leg and Ale Crock

serves 4

Ingredients

2 bottles amber ale
4 cups chicken bouillon
Legs of 4 pheasants
2 cups water
1 onion quartered
3 carrots, diced
4 medium potatoes, diced
2 tablespoons Worcestershire sauce
1 teaspoon celery salt
1 teaspoon salt
½ teaspoon pepper

For all the legs you are afraid to cook—be they from a wily rooster pheasant, a hill-climbing chukar, or a marathoner partridge—this is the cure. Don't get impatient; slow cooking in a crock is…slow…which is why it works.

COOKING

1. Pour the ale and bouillon into a slow cooker. Turn it on low and add the legs. Let the crock cook on low for 24 hours, until the meat is tender.
2. Remove the legs from the crock and pull the meat off the bones. Return the meat to the pot, with the water, onion, carrots, potatoes, Worcestershire sauce, celery salt, salt, and pepper. Cook on low another 4–6 hours.
3. Serve with homemade biscuits. ✹

Peasant Pheasant Pie

serves 4

Ingredients

FOR THE SOUP

½ cup minced onion
1 cup chopped celery
6 tablespoons butter or margarine
6 tablespoons flour
6 cups chicken bouillon
2 teaspoons fresh sage, minced (or 1 teaspoon dried leaf)
1 pound of pheasant breast meat (from 2 pheasants), diced
2 cups sliced carrot
2 cups corn (fresh or thawed)
2 cups peas (fresh or thawed)

FOR THE MASHED POTATO CRUST

6 medium potatoes, peeled and quartered
2 tablespoons butter
2 tablespoons sour cream
¾ cup milk
1 tablespoon chopped chives

Prepare this soup without the lid for lunch in the field or an easy Saturday night dinner, or go totally traditional with the mashed potato crust. Either way, you should use tender pheasant meat, or marinate it overnight in buttermilk to make it tender. This soup doesn't cook long enough to cure tough meat. For that, see the recipe that follows.

COOKING

1. Preheat the oven to 375°F. In a 5-quart Dutch oven, sauté the onion and celery in the butter over medium to medium-high heat until just tender, 3–4 minutes. One tablespoon at a time, sprinkle the flour over the sautéed vegetables, stirring each tablespoon until it is absorbed before adding the next. The last should make the mixture into a heavy paste. Immediately begin dribbling the chicken bouillon into the paste, stirring it in until the paste thins gradually into a sauce the consistency of ketchup.

2. Add the sage, pheasant meat, carrot, corn, and peas and bring the pot back to a low boil over high heat. Reduce the heat to simmer, cover, and cook another 20 minutes until the carrots are tender. Remove from heat while you make the crust. (You can even make the soup ahead, refrigerate it, and put the pie together later. A cool soup makes spreading the crust easier.)

3. To make a mashed potato crust: Boil the potatoes until tender and drain. Add the butter, sour cream, and milk, and mash the potatoes until they are smooth. Spread over the soup, sprinkle with the chives and bake at 375°F until the crust browns, about 30 minutes. (To get a rich brown you may have to turn the oven to broil for the last 5 minutes. Careful, or the crust will burn.) ❀

Rubbed Pheasant

serves 2

Ingredients

2 teaspoons brown sugar
1 teaspoon onion powder
½ teaspoon sweet paprika
½ teaspoon black pepper
⅛ teaspoon cayenne pepper
1 whole pheasant
2 tablespoons oil

Here's another way to barbecue whole birds, somewhat indirectly, by placing the bird on a rack in a drip pan. The fire can't reach the bird but the heat can, and the heat will sear the outside skin to preserve all those precious pheasant juices. Cook only until just done; more than that will fry all those delicious juices you were trying to catch.

PREPARATION

1. In a small bowl, combine the brown sugar, onion powder, paprika, black pepper, and cayenne pepper. Stir to mix the brown sugar into the spices thoroughly.
2. Trim and rinse the pheasant. Dry with paper towels. Rub the brown sugar mixture over the bird and press the spices into the skin with your fingers. Let the bird sit 10–15 minutes. Cover loosely with plastic wrap and refrigerate overnight.

COOKING

1. Preheat the barbecue to 400°F, about medium-low. (Double-check with an oven thermometer.)
2. When the barbecue is ready, place a poultry rack in an aluminum drip pan, and place the bird on the rack. Tie the legs together, tight up against the body (or see page 173 for fixing birds in the tuck position). Dribble the oil over the breast and legs. Place the pan in the center of the grill. Close the lid.
3. Roast the bird about 45–50 minutes until a meat thermometer registers 150°F when placed in the thigh. Or poke a hole in the rib meat; if the juices run clear or slightly pink, it's done.
4. Serve hot immediately, or chill 2–3 hours to serve with corn chips and salsa, and peppers. ⊛

Dry-Roasted Rooster

serves 2

Ingredients

3 tablespoons softened butter
1 tablespoon minced shallots
1 tablespoon Cognac
1 whole young pheasant (about 1¼ pounds oven-ready)

This may be dry roasting, but there's no reason for the bird to be dry. Before you stick this boy in the oven, check out page 173 and put his legs in the tuck position. This will ensure a good, moist leg when you least expect it.

COOKING

1. In a small skillet over medium heat, sauté the shallots in the butter until tender, about 3 minutes. Add the Cognac and cook another minute. Remove from heat. Transfer all the butter-Cognac mixture to a small cup, cover, and refrigerate 20 minutes, or until semisolid again.
2. Check the pheasant: Trim rough edges, pluck any remnant feathers, and clean the body cavity one more time. Rinse and pat dry with paper towels. With a spatula, spread the butter-Cognac over the pheasant, leaving a generous amount along the top of the sternum from belly to neck. (Just lay it on; it will all melt into the meat.) Let the bird sit for 20 minutes.
3. Preheat the oven to 350°F.
4. Place a poultry rack in a roasting pan, and put the pheasant breast side up on the rack. Position the roasting pan in center of the oven and roast about 35 minutes, basting every 10 minutes with the pan juices. The bird is done when a meat thermometer stuck in the thickest part of the thigh registers 150°F. Let the pheasant rest 10 minutes before carving. Serve with boiled red potatoes and green beans sautéed in a little butter and slivered almonds. Pour pan juices over the sliced bird. ◉

Traditional Marinated Roast Pheasant

serves 2

Ingredients

1 cup red wine (a Merlot or Cabernet is good)
¼ cup red wine vinegar
½ cup oil
2 cloves garlic, minced
3 green onions, chopped
10 whole allspice, cracked
1 teaspoon dried leaf sage
1 tablespoon plum preserves, liquefied
1 whole pheasant, skin on, legs tucked or tied together

For some, a pheasant isn't a pheasant until it's been marinated and dry roasted. Among that crowd half insist that you must leave the legs attached, the other half that you must remove them. This recipe is a compromise: it leaves the legs attached, but tucks them in tight to the body. The result is that instead of dry legs, they're moist. And both breast and legs, being pressed together, cook in about the same time.

PREPARATION

1. In a resealable plastic bag, combine the wine, vinegar, oil, garlic, green onion, allspice, sage, and plum preserves. Seal the bag and shake.
2. Trim and rinse the pheasant. Dry with paper towels and place in the bag with the marinade. Seal the bag, forcing as much air out as possible. Turn the bag several times to get the bird completely covered with the marinade. Let sit 24–48 hours in the refrigerator.

COOKING

1. Preheat oven to 350°F. Remove the bird from the marinade and pat dry. Save the marinade for basting.
2. Place the bird in a roasting pan with 2-inch sides. Baste with the marinade and place in the center of the oven. Roast about 45 minutes, basting at least two more times. The bird is done when a meat thermometer stuck into the inside of the thigh registers 150°F. Baste one more time when you take the bird out of the oven.
3. Let the bird sit 10 minutes to allow the juices to saturate the meat. Carve and arrange on a platter. If the pan juices are not burned, pour them over the sliced meat. Serve with mashed sweet potatoes and peas. ⊛

Wily Rooster Pot Roast

serves 2

Ingredients

2 ounces polish sausage, diced
2 tablespoons oil
1 cup Madeira
1 cup chicken bouillon
1 teaspoon dried leaf thyme
6 carrots, quartered
1 pound new red potatoes
1 pheasant

Here's the dish for that lucky hunter who manages to outwit the oldest, smartest rooster in the woods. You'll need it to cure what ails that bird. It works for almost any other wily old (read tough) bird you manage to put into your game bag.

COOKING

1. In a 5-quart Dutch oven, lightly brown the polish sausage over medium heat, about 5 minutes. Pour the Madeira into the pot, and stir up the tasty bits from the bottom. Let the Madeira come to a simmer, and simmer about 1 minute. Add the bouillon and thyme. Let this mixture come back to a simmer and lower the heat to medium-low. Preheat your oven to 300°F.

2. Add the carrots and potatoes, stirring them into the pan juices. Spread the vegetables to either side of the pot and nestle the pheasant into the pan juices. Spoon the sauce over the bird, too. Cover and place the Dutch oven in the center of the oven.

3. Let the pheasant cook about 60 minutes, or until the thighs are tender. To serve, carve the legs and breast off, and slice the breast across the grain. Arrange on a platter with the carrots and potatoes. Pour the pan juices over everything. ❀

Tasty Bits

Many years ago, I had the pleasure of spending a summer with some Australian students. In the course of this I learned many words—including "tasty bits." This term refers to the delicious, caramelized chunks of meat that invariably stick the bottom of the pan when you brown meats. (Good cast-iron pans help make them tasty bits and not charred remains!) Serious cooks refer to the process of adding liquid to gather these caramelized chunks as "deglazing the pan." However you refer to it, you don't want to relegate all this wonderful flavor to the dishwater.

Pheasant Kiev

serves 4

Ingredients

Boned breasts of 2 pheasants
1 cup buttermilk
½ cup butter (1 stick), softened
¼ cup minced fresh parsley
1 teaspoon chopped chives
½ teaspoon fresh thyme leaves
1 small clove garlic, minced
¼ teaspoon salt
⅛ teaspoon white pepper
2 tablespoons flour
1 egg, lightly beaten
2 tablespoons bread crumbs
Oil for deep-frying

Choose the best-looking pheasant breasts in the freezer and let the buttermilk—and butter—work their magic. You'll be amazed how tender and juicy those wily roosters can become.

PREPARATION

1. In a small resealable bag, marinate the breasts in the buttermilk for 24–48 hours in the refrigerator.
2. At the same time, prepare the seasoned butter. In a small bowl, combine the butter, parsley, chives, thyme, garlic, salt, and pepper. Stir well. Lay the seasoned butter on a piece of waxed paper or plastic wrap. Shape into a log about ½ inch in diameter. Wrap tightly and place in the freezer until quite hard, at least 1–2 hours.

COOKING

1. Drain and rinse the pheasant breasts. Pat dry. Lay the breasts on a piece of plastic wrap on top of a cutting board. With the palm of your hand press the thickest part of the breast, gently but firmly, until you feel it give but not tear. Continue pressing the thicker parts until the entire breast is fairly thin (about ¼ inch).
2. Slice the seasoned butter lengthwise and then crossways so you have four pieces. Place each section in the center of a flattened breasts. Roll up the breasts and secure the ends of each roll with toothpicks. Preheat the deep fryer. (A Fry Daddy will heat automatically to 360°–375°F, which is just right.)
3. Dredge each pheasant roll in flour, then egg, then breadcrumbs. Fry until dark golden brown, about 3–4 minutes each. Drain on paper towels until all the rolls are cooked. Serve with rice or boiled new potatoes tossed in butter and parsley. ⊛

South American Hoagie

serves 4

Ingredients

FOR THE MARINADE

⅓ cup olive oil
⅓ cup rice wine vinegar
1 tablespoon freshly squeezed lemon juice
⅓ cup diced onion
1 clove minced garlic
¼ teaspoon saffron threads
1 teaspoon fresh thyme leaves
¼ teaspoon salt
Breasts of 2 pheasants

FOR COOKING THE HOAGIE

1 medium Bermuda onion, sliced
1 red bell pepper, sliced
2 tablespoons oil
Loaf of Italian bread

Here's a dish no one will be able to pass up. Marinate the pheasant; then sauté it lightly with a pile of onions and peppers. This is a sandwich that does justice to pheasant—our favorite Chinese import, next to gun powder.

PREPARATION

1. In a resealable plastic bag, combine the oil, vinegar, lemon juice, onion, garlic, saffron, thyme, and salt. Shake well. Add the pheasant breasts and marinate in the refrigerator for 48 hours.
2. Pour off the marinade and discard it. Slice the pheasant meat across the grain in ¼-inch-thick strips.

ASSEMBLIING THE HOAGIE

1. Preheat the broiler and set a cooking rack approximately 4 inches below it. In a large saucepan, sauté the onion and red pepper in the oil over medium-high heat until they start to turn tender. Add the pheasant strips to the pan. Continue cooking, stirring often until the meat turns opaque (from red or pink to almost white), about 3–4 minutes.
2. Slice the Italian bread in half lengthwise and slice those halves in four equal lengths. Place them on a cookie sheet 3 inches under the broiler until browned, about 3 minutes. Remove the bread from the broiler, pile the pheasant-onion-pepper mixture on the bread, and serve. ✿

Heavenly Penne Casserole

serves 2–4

Ingredients

8 ounces penne pasta (or rigatoni, ziti, or
   any tube-shaped pasta)
1 cup minced onion
1 tablespoon oil
1 teaspoon dried leaf oregano
1 boned pheasant breast, diced
3 ounces diced ham
1 cup cream
8 ounces grated Swiss cheese

Here's a great cold-weather dish that you can make ahead of time and have ready to cook when you get home from work or play. Choose a tender pheasant or marinate tougher birds overnight in buttermilk to ensure good results.

COOKING

1. Start the pasta. Preheat oven to 375°F. In a large skillet, over medium heat, sauté the onion in oil until just tender, 3–4 minutes. Add the oregano and diced pheasant, stirring well. Sauté until the pheasant is cooked, 1–2 minutes. Add the ham and continue cooking until the ham is hot.

2. Drain the pasta and pour it into a lightly buttered 9-inch-square casserole dish. In the skillet, pour the cream over the pheasant mixture, stirring continually until the cream just comes to a low boil. Pour this mixture over the pasta with about half the cheese and mix thoroughly. Top the casserole with the rest of the cheese.

3. Bake in the oven for about 15 minutes, uncovered. Serve hot with fresh green beans on the side.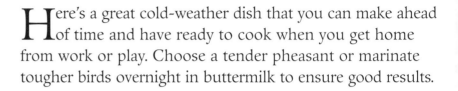

Chapter Four

Chukars, Hungarian Partridge, and Doves

Barbecued Whole Chukars

serves 6–8 people

Ingredients

12-ounce can ginger ale
4 whole chukars, plucked

BARBECUE SAUCE
¼ cup ketchup
⅛ cup apple cider vinegar
⅛ cup brown sugar
⅛ cup Worcestershire sauce
⅛ cup maple syrup
¼ cup mayonnaise

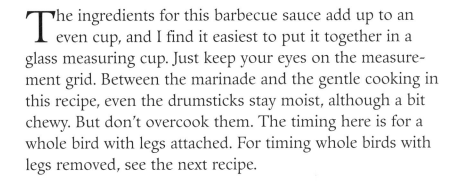

The ingredients for this barbecue sauce add up to an even cup, and I find it easiest to put it together in a glass measuring cup. Just keep your eyes on the measurement grid. Between the marinade and the gentle cooking in this recipe, even the drumsticks stay moist, although a bit chewy. But don't overcook them. The timing here is for a whole bird with legs attached. For timing whole birds with legs removed, see the next recipe.

PREPARATION
Pour the ginger ale into a 1-quart resealable plastic bag. Place the birds in the ginger ale. Seal and let marinate overnight in the refrigerator.

COOKING
1. In a glass measuring cup, combine the ketchup, vinegar, brown sugar, Worcestershire sauce, maple syrup, and mayonnaise. Stir well and set aside. Preheat your barbecue to about 400°F or medium. Set it for an indirect fire (see sidebar).
2. Remove the birds from the marinade and discard the marinade. When the barbecue is ready, place the birds on the cooking rack (but not directly over the heat), brush with the barbecue sauce, and close the lid.
3. Cook for about 50 to 55 minutes, basting 4 to 5 times

during the cooking, until a meat thermometer placed in the thigh (between thigh and breast, but into the thigh meat) registers 150°–155°F.

4. Let the birds sit at room temperature 8–10 minutes and then carve. I like to separate the legs at the hip joint and take the breast off whole. That way, I can cut the breast across the grain (see photos on page 170). ⊚

Cutting Across the Grain

Tenderness. It's a quality we want both in our bird dogs and our birds. But aren't birds either tender or tough before the shot? Yes, but you can improve them. Marinades help, as does aging. And for the breast, there's slicing across the grain. First, fillet the breast whole from the breastbone. Then turn the knife 90 degrees—so it lays across the length of the piece of breast. Since the grain runs the length of the muscle, slicing it this way cuts the grain, instead of paralleling it. It's the opposite of slicing the traditional, store-bought Thanksgiving turkey. There the bird is so tender, and so young, you can slice with the grain—as jerky-makers do to preserve the texture—and not have to chew any harder. But with wild birds...the difference can be quite noticeable.

Grilling with an Indirect Fire

To set an indirect fire on two-burner propane grills, light one side and place the food to be grilled on the other side. For charcoal grills, start the fire in the middle of the fire rack. When the charcoal is ready, move half the coals to one side and half to the other, leaving a space in the middle of the grill where the birds will not be sitting directly over the hot coals. This way you have heat but no fire directly below the bird. As a result, the meat cooks evenly, and you don't have to turn it several times or fight fat flare-ups.

Easy Bacon Breast

serves 2

Ingredients

1 whole chukar with skin on, legs removed at the hip joint
1 slice bacon

This may be the easiest and fastest way to gnaw on a delicious chunk of grilled chukar—or any other bird for that matter. I don't know too many birds that don't improve with a little fat. This recipe is timed for a bit higher heat; with no legs to slow down the process, the heat goes directly to the breast meat.

COOKING

1. Preheat your grill to 375°–400°F, setting an indirect fire (see "Grilling with an Indirect Fire" under previous recipe).
2. Rinse, dry, and trim the bird, removing any rough edges that will scorch and burn. Cut the bacon in half, then place both pieces across the breastbone so that most of the meat is covered. Place the bird on the cooking surface away from the fire and close the lid.
3. Cook for about 25 to 30 minutes; hot summer days will not affect the temperature, but cool autumn and cold winter days may add some cooking time. Check with a meat thermometer in the thickest part of the breast, being careful not to touch bone. When inserted, the juices should run clear (no pink at all) and the internal temperature should be about 160°F. The outer temperature will be enough hotter to cook the bacon completely.
4. Serve hot or cold with peach chutney. ❁

Chukar Italiano

serves 4

Ingredients

1 cup chopped onion
2 teaspoons diced garlic
2 tablespoons oil
1 14.5-ounce can whole peeled tomatoes
1 tablespoon chopped fresh basil (or 1 teaspoon dried leaf)
2 teaspoons capers, drained
1 tablespoon chopped black olives
Boned breasts of 2 chukars, sliced across the grain
½ teaspoon salt
¼ teaspoon pepper

A robust, flavorful dish with the meat of one of the West's best-kept secrets. If you don't have chukars, you can substitute any tender, white-meated bird. Quail will work, as will grouse; just be sure to have about 6–8 ounces (1–1½ cups) of boned meat to fill out this dish.

COOKING

1. In a large skillet, sauté the onion and garlic in oil over medium heat until they begin to brown, about 5 minutes. Add the tomatoes, breaking them up in the skillet.
2. Once the tomatoes start to simmer, add the basil, capers, olives, sliced chukar, salt, and pepper. Reduce the heat to low, cover the skillet, and simmer about 10 minutes. Serve over pasta, or with garlic bread. ✸

Elegant Chukar in Champagne and Pear Sauce

serves 2

Ingredients

2 tablespoons butter
Boned breasts of 2 chukars
1 Bosc pear, peeled, cored, and sliced lengthwise
2 tablespoons fresh thyme
½ cup brut champagne
¼ teaspoon salt
⅛ teaspoon white pepper

Perfect for the delicate white meat of chukar partridge, this Champagne and Pear Sauce is quietly unassuming. Try it on grouse and quail, too, if you're looking for something that won't overwhelm these white-fleshed birds.

COOKING

1. In a large skillet, melt the butter over medium heat. While it melts, dry the meat with paper towels. When the butter just begins to sizzle, add the breasts and sauté until they just begin to brown, about 1 minute a side. Remove the breasts and cover with foil to keep warm.

2. Gently place the pear slices into the hot butter. Sprinkle with the thyme and sauté until the pear is quite soft, about 3 minutes. Turn them gently once with a spatula, but don't stir.

3. Add the champagne, salt, and pepper. Continue to cook, letting the champagne simmer until it reduces by about half, 4–5 minutes.

4. Return the breasts to the skillet, spoon the sauce over them, and cover the skillet. Continue cooking 3–4 more minutes until the breasts are hot again. Serve immediately with fresh asparagus spears. ◉

Chukar Egg Rolls

makes 8 full-sized egg rolls

Ingredients

FOR THE DIPPING SAUCE

1 tablespoon soy sauce
2 tablespoons rice wine vinegar
½ teaspoon grated fresh ginger
½ teaspoon sugar
2 teaspoons water

FOR THE EGG ROLLS

½ cup (3 ounces) ground pork
Breast of 1 chukar, boned and thinly sliced
2 tablespoons oil, in all
1 cup grated carrots
1 cup thinly sliced onion
2 cups thinly sliced Napa cabbage
1 tablespoon soy sauce
8 egg roll wrappers

You can make these egg rolls with almost any pale- to medium-fleshed bird. Use the leftovers of a dry-roasted turkey or simply slice up a boned breast. Just be sure to have about a half of a pound of meat (about 1⅛ cups) for the filling. Oh, and the sauce. This is a very pungent dipping sauce, and it's very easy to make. But you can use a prepared sweet-and-sour sauce, or Chinese hot mustard.

PREPARATION

1. Combine the soy sauce, rice vinegar, ginger, sugar, and water in a small bowl. Set aside.
2. In a large skillet, sauté the pork and chukar breast meat in 1 tablespoon of the oil, over medium-high heat until they are cooked through but not browned, about 3–4 minutes. Add the carrots, onion, and cabbage and sauté until they wilt, about 2–3 minutes. Add the soy sauce, and stir to coat all the ingredients. Remove from heat and cool at room temperature.

COOKING

1. To make the egg rolls, preheat a deep-fat fryer to 375°F. Or pour 3 inches of oil in a Dutch oven and heat to 375°F. If you have a metal cake cooling rack, set it on the counter nearby with paper towels under it and use it to drain the egg rolls. Otherwise, a platter covered with plenty of paper towels will also work.
2. Lay out an egg roll wrapper on a cutting board so that it looks like a baseball diamond, with home plate closest to you. Spoon ¼ cup of the cabbage mixture into the center of the wrapper. Fold home plate over the filling, and then roll the wrapper halfway up. Fold over 1st and 3rd base. Moisten

second base with a bit of cold water and roll the egg roll the rest of the way closed.

3. When you're done rolling and the oil is at 375°F, start cooking. Carefully drop the egg rolls in one at a time, leaving lots of room around each. (In a Fry Daddy you'll only be able to cook 2–3 at a time; in a Dutch oven, probably 4–5. Just leave space for the oil to get completely around the wrapper.)

4. Cook about 4 minutes each until golden brown. Drain on paper towels or the cake rack. Eat while hot, with the dipping sauce.

Tip

There are usually between 19 and 20 egg roll wrappers to a package. This recipe calls for 8, which is enough food for 4 people. If you want to make the entire package of egg roll wrappers, simply double this recipe. That will still leave you one or two wrappers in case something goes wrong.

Quick-As-A-Chukar Chili

serves 4

Ingredients

1 pound boned chukar meat, cut in thin, 1½-inch-long strips
3 tablespoons oil, in all
½ medium yellow onion, sliced
1 15-ounce can black beans, drained and rinsed
1 cup corn
1 cup mild bottled salsa
½ teaspoon chopped red jalapeño pepper
½ teaspoon ground cumin

On Chili Peppers

Like snowflakes, no two chili peppers are alike. That is true whether you use store-bought or homegrown chili peppers, and the results of miscalculation can be disastrous. When preparing chilies for cooking, first cut them in half lengthwise and remove the seeds and any part of the inside core that is pale or white. This is the hottest part of the chili. Then cut up the amount you want to use and add it the dish gradually, tasting the result as you go. For quick stove-to-table dishes like this one, you can keep close tabs on the heat. For long-cooking dishes, or when you make enough for several meals, you'll need to back off a bit.

Jalapeños get hotter—even in the freezer—the longer they're allowed to sit.

Another of John's lunch inventions, this chili is as quick as it gets, and it sticks to your ribs when you're planning a long walk in the woods. Use any boned meat—from the chukar suggested here to the ugliest prairie grouse—and feel free to use hot salsa if that's what you prefer. As it's written, this chili barks pretty loud, but it doesn't bite.

COOKING

1. In a large skillet, sauté the meat in 2 tablespoons of the oil over medium-high heat until lightly browned, about 5 minutes. In a second skillet, sauté the onion in the rest of the oil, over medium heat until it is lightly browned, as well. Combine in one skillet.

2. To this skillet, add the beans, corn, salsa, red jalapeño pepper, and cumin. Stir well to combine. Let the skillet come to a low simmer, reduce the heat to low, and cover. Continue cooking for 8–10 minutes until all the ingredients are hot and the flavors have had a chance to mix.

3. Serve immediately with frozen tortillas that have been crisped in your toaster. (Set the toaster on low-medium setting. The tortillas may need 1½ cycles to thaw and crisp. Be sure to remove any frost from your tortillas before inserting them in the toaster.) ◉

Four-Can Crock

serves 2–4

Ingredients

2 cans lite beer
1 15-ounce can stewed tomatoes
1 6-ounce can tomato paste
1½ teaspoons salt
½ teaspoon coarse black pepper
⅓ cup sour cream
Breasts and legs of 2 chukars

I don't know what's easier than this except, perhaps, going out to eat. The trick is to throw in as few small bones as possible since they'll be floating and hard to find by the time this crock is done. So bone the breast or pull the breast—with sternum attached—from the rest of the rib cage. Then separate the legs from the carcass at the hip joint. (See page 159 for details.) All you have left are a few large bones.

COOKING

1. Pour the beer, stewed tomatoes, tomato paste, salt, pepper, and sour cream into a 5-quart slow cooker. Stir well to mix the ingredients. Now add the chukars.
2. Cook on medium for 6 to 8 hours or until the meat is falling off the bones. Serve over rice. ❀

Sauer Chukar Soup

serves 4

Ingredients

2 slices bacon, chopped
1 onion, chopped
2 boned chukar breasts, diced
7 medium-sized potatoes, diced
1 cup apple cider vinegar
¼ cup brown sugar
2 tablespoons chicken bouillon granules
6 cups hot water
½ red cabbage, chopped
1 grated potato

This is a good soup for odds and ends of various birds—from pheasant to sharp-tailed grouse—anything you don't know what the heck to do with. And no, the "sauer" does not refer to the meat going bad. It's the classic German "sour" sauce. Here I've used chukar because that's what we had the most of, left over in the freezer from last year. Use any bird you've got hanging around. The sauer sauce hides a lot of sins.

COOKING

1. In a 5-quart Dutch oven, sauté the bacon over medium heat until it is browned and fairly crisp. Add the chopped onion and breast meat. Stir to cover with the pan juices. Continue cooking, stirring often, until the onions are tender, about 4–5 minutes. Add the diced potatoes and toss all the ingredients together until the potatoes are covered in the pan juices.

2. Combine the cider vinegar with the brown sugar, stir, and add to the Dutch oven. Stir to coat the onions, meat, and potatoes. Let the vinegar cook down until the pot is almost dry. Combine the chicken bouillon granules and water, mix well, and when diluted add this to the pot. Stir and raise the heat to medium-high, letting the pot come to a slow boil. Cover and cook about 30 minutes.

3. Add the cabbage and grated potato to the Dutch oven, stirring well to mix all the ingredients together. Lower the heat to simmer and continue cooking another 10 minutes. Serve with hard rolls. ☉

Tip

There are lots of ways to thicken soups: adding a little cornstarch mixed with cold water, dredging the meat in flour before browning, or even breaking up a slice of good brown bread across the top of the soup as it's finishing cooking. That last is a Dutch method, and I don't use it often because it's hard to find a good brown bread in my neighborhood.

Potatoes, however, are easy to find and work just as well. You may need to use caution, however: Fine grating releases all the potato's starch, freeing it to turn the thinnest of soups into thick stews in less time than it takes to set the table. One medium potato is plenty of starch for this recipe. The result won't be quite as thick as turkey gravy, but it will be close.

UPLAND GAME COOKERY

Quick-Grilled Hungarian Legs

serves 2

Ingredients

½ teaspoon ground cumin
½ teaspoon onion powder
¼ teaspoon chili powder
¼ teaspoon salt
Legs of 8 Hungarian partridges, skin on or off
1 tablespoon oil

Hungarian partridge often get a bad rap for dry, stringy legs. But cooked quickly over low heat on the grill, their legs make a juicy, tender tidbit for appetizers or, if you're lucky and have plenty, an entire meal. Use thighs and drumsticks—attached or unattached. They will cook in about the same time and the drumsticks will be tender, too. Just follow the directions and use your best-looking Huns.

COOKING

1. Preheat your grill to low heat, about 300°F at the cooking surface. (Use a common oven thermometer to check your grill. With two-burner propane units, use only one burner; with both burners, even the lowest setting will usually rise above 300°F.) Combine the cumin, onion powder, chili powder, and salt in a small bowl or a salt shaker.
2. Trim and rinse the legs. Dry with paper towels and spread out in a single layer on a platter. Sprinkle the spice mix on both sides of the legs, and press into the flesh with your fingers.
3. When the grill is ready, wipe a bit of oil on the legs. Place them on the grill and close the lid. Let the legs cook about 7–8 minutes, turning once halfway through. Remove from heat and eat immediately. ◉

Tip

To make that last-minute job of brushing the bird with oil a bit easier, I use a squeeze bottle—like the tall plastic ketchup and mustard dispensers found in hamburger joints. You can also use a small bowl and pastry brush if you've got them in your kitchen drawer already, but the squeeze bottle is pretty handy at the grill. Fill it at least half full, and it won't tip over on windy afternoons.

Indirectly, Whole Hungarians

serves 2

Ingredients

1½ teaspoons onion powder
½ teaspoon salt
½ teaspoon ground cumin
¼ teaspoon chili powder
⅛ teaspoon white pepper
⅛ teaspoon garlic powder
⅛ teaspoon sweet paprika
⅛ teaspoon sugar
2 whole Hungarian partridge, skin on
2 tablespoons oil

The secret to roasting a whole bird on a grill is indirect cooking (setting the fire on one end of the barbecue, your food on the other), as described on page 59. This cooking method and timing will work for other Hun-sized birds: namely, chukars, ruffed grouse, and spruce grouse (all three slightly larger but mild in flavor). But neither this nor the grilled recipe that comes

before will cure gamy flavors. So, if the bird smells gamy, look for other, more highly spiced recipes.

COOKING

1. Preheat your barbecue to medium-low, about 400°F. (Use a common oven thermometer to double check your grill.) In a small bowl or salt shaker, combine the onion powder, salt, cumin, chili powder, white pepper, garlic powder, paprika, and sugar. Stir or shake to mix.
2. Trim and rinse the birds. Dry inside and out with paper towels. Set the birds on a platter or cutting board. Sprinkle the spice mix over the birds, pressing it into the skin with your fingers. Rub the oil all over the skin.
3. When the fire is ready and set up for indirect cooking, place the birds on the unlit area of the grill breast up and close the lid. Cook 20 minutes at 400°F. Remove when done; a meat thermometer placed in the thickest part of the thigh will read 150°F still hot from the grill.
4. Slice, taking the legs off at the hip joint and slicing the breast meat vertically, giving each slice a bit of the spice-encrusted skin. Serve with coleslaw and a fresh garden salad. ✺

Posh Partridge

serves 2

Ingredients

2 cloves garlic, minced
2 tablespoons butter
4 ounces mushrooms, sliced
Boned breasts of 2 Hungarian partridge, sliced across the grain
¼ cup medium-dry sherry

There's something very attractive about a dinner that cooks in 10 minutes. It borders on nirvana when that dish not only provides a quick weeknight dinner but a Saturday night get-together to impress your friends. Use Hungarian partridge as I've done here, or whatever is in your freezer. The robust flavors of garlic, sherry, and mushrooms can handle all but the gamiest meat. (For those, see the ginger ale marinade in the Barbecued Whole Chukar recipe on page 58).

COOKING

1. In a large skillet, gently sauté the garlic in butter over medium heat, about 2–3 minutes. Add the mushrooms and gently toss them lightly in the butter and garlic. When the butter starts sizzling again, add the sliced meat. Stir to coat the meat. Cook 3–4 minutes until all the butter has been absorbed.
2. Slowly drizzle the sherry across the whole pan. When it comes to a slow simmer, turn the heat down to medium-low. Continue cooking until there is very little liquid left in the pan. Serve immediately over egg noodles. ◉

Surfin' Hungarians

serves 2

Ingredients

FOR THE SQUASH
1 whole acorn squash
1 tablespoon butter or margarine

FOR THE HUNS
¼ cup frozen orange juice concentrate, thawed but not diluted
¼ cup coconut milk
2 teaspoons grated fresh ginger
Breasts of 2 Hungarian partridge
6 large shrimp (about 4 ounces)
1 tablespoon butter
2 green onions, chopped, white and green parts separated

Here's one for special occasions! A rich, Polynesian-style blend of surf and sky that will spark up a winter's night. The best part is that it's easy. When you put the squash in the oven, start the meat marinating. By the time the squash is done, the rest of the dish will be ready. Feel free to substitute any bird with pale to medium-pale flesh. (Squash-haters can substitute rice. It's really all about the sauce!)

COOKING

1. Preheat the oven to 350°F. Cut the acorn squash in half, across the middle (not through the stem). Scoop out the seeds and loose pulp with a table spoon, and turn open side down on a cutting board. Slice off enough of the stem end and the top so that the squash "bowls" will sit on a baking pan without tipping. Be careful not to make a hole in the bowl.

2. Brush the inside of the squash with the butter and place on a baking pan. Bake in the center of the oven for 45 minutes.

3. In a large bowl, combine the orange juice concentrate, coconut milk, and ginger. Stir well. Add the cubed Hungarian partridge meat and the shrimp to the orange juice. Toss to coat everything. Set aside at room temperature for 20 minutes.

4. Pull the shrimp from the marinade and set them aside for the moment. Melt the butter in a 9-inch skillet over medium heat. Add the minced whites of the green onions to the butter and sauté 1 minute until they start to sizzle. Pour the Huns with all the marinade into the skillet and cook over medium heat, stirring constantly to keep the meat coated. Let the Huns cook 3–4 minutes. Add the shrimp to the pan and cook another 2–3 minutes until the shrimp turn pink.

5. Place the squash bowls on plates, and divide the shrimp and Hun mixture into the two bowls. Garnish with the minced greens of the green onion. Serve with a good pilsner beer. ◉

Creamed Cajun Casserole

serves 2

Ingredients

¼ teaspoon dried leaf thyme
¼ teaspoon dried leaf oregano
¼ teaspoon sweet paprika
⅛ teaspoon garlic salt
⅛ teaspoon black pepper
⅛ teaspoon white pepper
Pinch of cayenne pepper
½ cup chopped onion
½ cup chopped celery
½ green pepper, chopped
1 tablespoon oil
Legs and breasts of 4 Hungarian partridge
½ cup chicken broth
1 14.75-ounce can creamed corn

A simple throw-together dish that becomes something special in the oven, and a delicious favorite on the plate. Use any parts you want, legs or breasts, and any bird you want from pale to dark. One of my favorites is Hungarian partridge. The magic is that 90 minutes of moist cooking in the oven turns even tough old drumsticks into tender morsels.

COOKING

1. Preheat oven to 375°F. Measure out the thyme, oregano, paprika, garlic salt, black pepper, white pepper, and cayenne into a small bowl. In a 2-quart Dutch oven, sauté the onion, celery, and green pepper in oil over medium-high heat until the vegetables start to brown, about 5 minutes.
2. Add the spice mix and stir it into the vegetables. Once you start to smell the spices, nestle the legs into the bottom of the skillet. Do not brown the legs.
3. Pour the chicken broth over the legs and spoon the creamed corn over the entire dish. Cover and place in the center of the oven.
4. Bake for 90 minutes. Serve immediately with toasted tortillas and a green salad. ❁

September Partridge Stew

serves 4

Ingredients

1 yellow onion, sliced thin
2 cloves garlic, minced
Boned breasts of 3 Hungarian partridge
2 tablespoons oil
2 cups chopped crookneck squash (or other yellow squash)
2 teaspoons dried leaf thyme
2 bay leaves
1 teaspoon salt
½ teaspoon pepper
4 cups chicken bouillon
2 cups diced ripe tomatoes
2 cups diced potatoes
½ cup grated Parmesan cheese

Every September, as the garden winds down, there's always a glut of one thing or another. This year it was crookneck squash and one tomato plant that ripened very late. By then I was in the mood for hunting not gathering, and that's how the harvest stew went this year.

COOKING

1. In a medium-hot skillet, sauté the onion, garlic, and breast meat in the oil until the meat is lightly browned. Add the squash and continue cooking until the squash gets brighter in color, about 4–5 minutes. Add the thyme, bay leaves, salt, and pepper. Stir the spices into the browned meat and vegetables.

2. When you begin to smell the herbs and spices, add the bouillon, tomatoes, and potatoes. Bring the skillet up to a low simmer and reduce the heat to low. Cover the pot and simmer 45 minutes or until the meat and potatoes are tender.

3. To serve, sprinkle liberally with Parmesan cheese. ◉

Save-The-Legs Three-Onion Crock

serves 4–6

Ingredients

1–2 pounds mixed upland bird legs
1 red onion, sliced thin
1 yellow onion, sliced thin
2 tablespoons oil
1 teaspoon sugar
1 tablespoon dried onion flakes
¼ cup Marsala wine
2 cups chicken bouillon
1 teaspoon summer savory
¼ teaspoon white pepper
¼ teaspoon black pepper
1 pound frozen pearl onions, thawed
1 cup white, wild, or brown rice (or mixed)

This recipe makes a delicious soup. Or you can use the preparation steps (and all the ingredients but the pearl onions and rice) as the first step to transform the drumsticks of any birds—including pheasants, prairie grouse, and chukars—into soup meat. Once the slow cooker has done its work, pull the meat from the bones and add it to any of the soup recipes in this book. You can also add the broth; just substitute this cooked broth for an equal amount of uncooked bouillon in your recipe.

PREPARATION

1. Sauté the legs and sliced red and yellow onion in the oil and sugar over medium heat. When the legs are lightly browned and the onions starting to brown, add the onion flakes, Marsala, chicken bouillon, summer savory, white pepper, and black pepper. Stir to coat all the ingredients with the herbs. Continue cooking on medium heat until you begin to smell the herbs, about 3–4 minutes.
2. Transfer to a slow cooker and cover. Turn the slow cooker on medium and cook about 7–24 hours—long enough for the leg meat to fall off the bones. Remove the legs from the pot and let them cool. Pull the meat off the bones and remove the tendons from the meat. (Stop here if you intend to add this leg meat to another soup recipe.) Return the meat to the slow cooker.

COOKING

1. Turn the slow cooker up to high and add the pearl onions and rice. Cover.
2. Once the mixture comes to a low boil, let it cook on high for about 1 hour. ◉

B&B Prairie Stew

serves 2–4

Ingredients

8 ounces mixed Hungarian partridge and sharptail breast meat
   (about 1⅓ cups), cut in bite-sized pieces
2 cups minced onion
2 tablespoons oil
1 teaspoon dried leaf sage
1 teaspoon celery salt
1 teaspoon salt
½ teaspoon pepper
2 12-ounce beers
4 teaspoons chicken bouillon granules
2 cups hot water
2 cups chopped carrots
½ cup barley

No, this recipe doesn't come from a quaint New England inn. This B&B is beer and barley, two of my favorite soup ingredients. The barley is a stick-to-your-ribs grain. And the beer? It helps tenderize any bird you want to put in the pot. Here, I'm using a combination of Hungarian partridge and sharptails.

COOKING

1. In a 5-quart Dutch oven, over medium-high heat, sauté the meat and onions in the oil until they start to brown. Add the sage, celery salt, salt, pepper, and stir to coat. When you begin to smell the seasonings, slowly add the beer. Bring the pot to a low boil and mix together the bouillon granules and water until well dissolved. Add that to the pot with the carrots and the barley. Stir and bring the pot back to a low boil.

2. Cover and lower the heat to simmer. Cook about 45 minutes until the barley and carrots are cooked. Serve with cold beer.

3. Alternately, once the pot comes back to a simmer, you can transfer the Dutch oven to a 200°F oven and go hunting for 2–3 hours. Your dinner will be ready when you get home. ✹

Buttermilk Doves

serves 4

Ingredients

8–10 whole doves, plucked
1 cup buttermilk
4–5 slices bacon

Doves are one of those borderline game birds that some people love and others find just a bit on the gamy side. Whichever side you're on, an overnight soak in buttermilk makes them even better. The milk part of buttermilk mellows flavor; the acid tenderizes the meat. And don't stop with doves. Buttermilk will tenderize and mellow any bird you find either tough or gamy.

PREPARATION

Rinse and dry the doves carefully. Trim rough edges. Place in a resealable plastic bag and pour the buttermilk over the birds. Close the bag and shake. Marinate the birds overnight in the refrigerator.

COOKING

1. Preheat a barbecue grill to low, about 300°F. Pour off the buttermilk marinade and rinse the birds. Pat dry inside and out with paper towels.
2. Cut bacon slices in half and wrap each half around a bird. Secure with toothpicks.
3. Place the doves on the grill. Cook slowly, turning from side to side every 10 minutes, finishing with the breast down. The birds are done when the bacon is browned but not black. Serve immediately. ◉

Quick-Draw Doves

serves 4–6

Ingredients

9 doves, plucked
2 tablespoons diced beef suet
2 tablespoons butter
1 large onion, chopped
1 teaspoon dried leaf sage
1 cup cooked lima beans
6 large carrots
1 head cabbage, cut into 8 pieces
2 cups beef bouillon
3 cups cooked egg noodles

According to the late George Leonard Herter, catalog magnate, Wyatt Earp was once asked, "What's the best shot you ever made?" Earp allegedly responded, "Nine doves with one shot." I would have liked to have seen that, and I would have liked to have been in the kitchen when he cooked them up because, again according to Herter, Earp was a gourmet cook. This recipe is reported to have been one of Wyatt's concoctions for just such a 9-dove morning. A century later it's still a great way to cook dark-fleshed birds.

COOKING

1. Rinse, trim, and dry the doves inside and out. Set aside. In a 3- to 5-quart Dutch oven, render the beef suet slowly over low heat. When the suet is liquefied, add the butter and raise the heat to medium.
2. Add the onions and doves to the suet. Sauté until the birds are lightly browned and the onions softened. Add the sage, lima beans, carrots, cabbage, and bouillon. (You should have about 2 inches of liquid in the pot. If not, add more bouillon.) Bring the pot back to a simmer and cover. Cook at a low simmer for about 90 minutes.
3. To serve, place the noodles onto a platter and arrange the vegetables and doves around them. Pour the pan juices over the top. ⊛

Tip

Herter fans will notice I cooked this a bit differently from George's directions. I prefer sautéed onions to boiled, and bouillon to plain water as a stock. Since George didn't hear this recipe from the horse's mouth, I figure that's OK. The results are spectacular. This is one of those dishes that fills the house with good old home-cooking aromas and drives you crazy waiting for it to be done.

Slow-Grilled Doves

serves 3-4

Ingredients

¼ cup margarine, melted
2 tablespoons soy sauce
2 tablespoons Worcestershire sauce
2 tablespoons lemon juice
2 tablespoons apple cider vinegar
2 cloves garlic, minced
1 orange, peeled and seeded
½ teaspoon pepper
Merlot or Beaujolais to cover
12 doves, cleaned and plucked
6 slices bacon

Aaron Pass is not only a friend, but he has a way with the grill. This is his recipe, and in offering it to us, he warns that the fire must be set fairly low on the grill—and the cooking surface raised as high as possible. His guide is how long it takes to cook these little doves: The fire should be slow enough or far enough from the birds to cook them in no less than 45 to 60 minutes. The longer it takes, the better the results. (I find a good test is to place the marinade in a cast-iron pot on the cooking surface. A very gentle simmer for the marinade, makes for good dove cooking.) Aaron also points out that this marinade works on almost any bird, and even venison.

PREPARATION

1. Combine the margarine, soy sauce, Worcestershire, lemon juice, vinegar, and garlic in a noncorrosive bowl. Chop the orange—pulp and all—and add it to the marinade.
2. Dry the doves inside and out with paper towels and add the birds to the marinade. Add enough red wine to cover them. Cover the bowl and marinate in the refrigerator 8–24 hours, depending on whether you want a mild or strong flavor.

COOKING

1. Pour the marinade off into a small cast-iron saucepan, (or a deep and narrow saucepan you can safely use on the barbecue). Preheat the barbecue to medium-low heat, 300°–325°F on an oven thermometer.
2. While the barbecue heats up, wrap each bird in half a slice of bacon. Then test the grill. Place the marinade saucepan in the center of the cooking surface; it should come to a very low simmer, creating just a few bubbles at a time. Lower the heat if necessary.
3. When the heat is right, start the birds. Dip each bird in the marinade and place breast up on the grill. Close the grill and set a timer for 15 minutes. Watch for fat flare-ups.

4. Turn the birds every 15 minutes, dipping them in the marinade and rotating them each time: First breast up, then one wing up, next the second wing up, and finally breast side down. When the bacon is done, the birds will also be done. Remove from the grill and serve hot with baked beans. ⊛

Tip

Aaron prefers to use charcoal for this recipe, and a kettle-style grill is best for keeping fat flare-ups under control. I prefer the speed of propane, so I tried that. Problem is, propane is meant to blister. Getting it choked down to slow-cooking temperature is a delicate operation. Begin by preheating at the lowest setting you have. Then, if that's not 300°–325°F, which it probably won't be, start closing the valve on the tank to reduce the available fuel. Place an oven thermometer on the cooking surface, and test how low you can go. Then, since propane barbecues have lots of air leaks, keep a water pistol handy to put out the inevitable flare-ups. A propane barbecue will work, but a charcoal grill is a lot easier to control.

Baked Doves

serves 2–4

Ingredients

½ cup Dijon mustard
¼ cup honey
2 apricots, pitted
¼–½ cup dry white wine
9–12 dove breasts

Here's an easy recipe that shines on cold wintry nights. I like to use dove breasts that have been skinned and "pulled" from the carcass with the sternum attached, à la quail (see details on pages 162–164). Whole birds will work just as well, with or without skin. The beauty of the sauce is that it goes with a variety of birds—from doves to the palest of mountain grouse.

COOKING

1. Preheat the oven to 325°F. In a small blender, combine the mustard, honey, and apricots and purée. Arrange the dove breasts in an 8- to 10-inch covered 3-quart casserole. (The size of the casserole and the number of birds are interdependent: the birds need to be in a single layer, but cheek to cheek.)

2. Add ¼ cup of the white wine to the sauce and pour it over the birds. Add as much as another ¼ cup of the wine if necessary to cover.

3. Cover the casserole and place in the center of the oven. Bake 45 minutes. Serve hot with wild and white rice mixed half and half. ❁

Tip

You can assemble this dish several hours in advance and place the casserole in the refrigerator to marinate, even overnight. When you're ready to cook, just put it in the oven.

Chapter Five

Prairie Chickens, Sharp-tailed Grouse, Sage Grouse, and Woodcock

There's a very good reason these four birds are grouped together. Of all the wild birds we hunt, these four are the ones most people admit they don't really enjoy eating. The three prairie birds can also be the most variable in flavor depending on how old the bird is, how fast you draw and cool them in the field, how you cook them, and how long you cook them. They can be just as delicious as the best pheasant, or they can be all but inedible.

At our house, we know young birds are better than old ones, unstressed better than stressed, early season better than late. I once tried to prove that corn-fed Nebraskan sharptails taste better than Montana's sagebrush sharptails without much luck. One day in Nebraska, I found every sharptail we had taken had a different food in its craw: corn in one, rose hips in another, grasshoppers in a third, and so on. One sharptail's craw was completely empty. It was immediately apparent that had we done the same test the day before—or after—bird three would have eaten bird two's breakfast, bird two, bird three's breakfast, and bird one would have snuck back in the farmyard and pigged out on Purina cat chow.

For most upland birds there is no danger in waiting until some February night to prepare the white wine marinade. With these prairie birds, that isn't soon enough. Starting right after the shot, you need to keep the bad flavors from percolating into the meat. What I have found over the years is that a three-prong attack works best to stop bad flavors: (1) drawing and rinsing the birds as soon as possible, (2) tossing salt in the mature male's body cavity, and (3) icing the entire bird inside and out—more ice than for the other upland birds. (For details on field care, see chapter 8)

Why have the venerable woodcock been lumped in with the prairie birds? It's the flavor. Many people find that woodcock taste "livery," just as many people find prairie birds "strong." I find that woodcock

Chukar Italiano

recipe on page 61

Barbecued
Whole Chukars

recipe on page 58

Elegant Chukar
in Champagne
and Pear Sauce

recipe on page 62

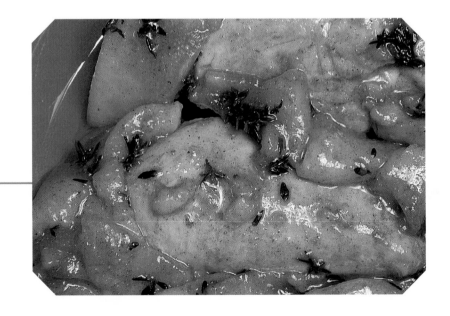

Chukar Egg Rolls

recipe on page 63

Surfin' Hungarians

recipe on page 72

Quick-Grilled
Hungarian Legs

recipe on page 69

Posh Partridge

recipe on page 71

B&B Prairie Stew

recipe on page 76

Quick-Draw Doves

recipe on page 78

September Partridge Stew

recipe on page 74

Slow-Cooked
Sharptail Pockets

recipe on page 90

Maple-Smoked
Sharptails

recipe on page 91

Caesar Salad à la Woodcock

recipe on page 102

Robert P's Sautéed Turkey Breast

recipe on page 109

Woodcock
Want-Nots

recipe on page 100

Sage Grouse
Stroganoff

recipe on page 96

John's
Ten-Minute Soup

recipe on page 105

Un-Traditional Fourth
of July Fried Turkey

recipe on page 114

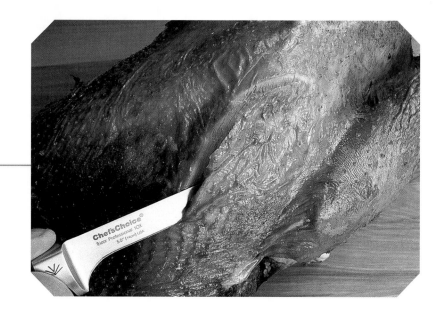

Traditional Sage Breakfast Sausage

recipe on page 129

Turkey Nuggets

recipe on page 111

Turkey Chow Mein

recipe on page 113

Bird Brats

recipe on page 133

Italian Garden Sausage

recipe on page 131

Smoked
Summer Sausage

recipe on page 137

only taste "livery" when overcooked or reheated. Leave them slightly pink inside and you'll find the flavor mild. Some compare it to the taste of fine beef. Take them past medium so that all the pink is gone, and you'll notice the "livery" off-flavor. (Oddly, I've found that ruffed grouse suffer a similar change in flavor when overcooked or reheated.) The change takes place quickly—often in just a minute or two—so monitor the cooking time very carefully. Rare is good; overdone can be disastrous.

The same holds true for cooking the prairie birds. Overcooking sage grouse, for example, can create an almost chemical taste. Cook delicately. A little pink is good. It means there's more moisture, too, and my own theory is that cooking out all the moisture just concentrates bad flavors enough so we notice them more.

Cooked properly, all of these game birds can have wonderful tastes that are distinctive of wild birds.

Pop-Kabobs

serves 8

Ingredients

Boned breasts of 4 sharp-tailed grouse (or prairie chickens)
1 12-ounce can ginger ale
1 green bell pepper
1 medium yellow onion
8 strips bacon
1 teaspoon salt
½ teaspoon black pepper
1 teaspoon dried leaf basil
8 kabob skewers

You'll need to start this marinade a few days ahead of time. I've soaked the breasts for as long as 4 days in the ginger ale, but 3 is enough to really tenderize and mellow out these wild plains birds.

PREPARATION

1. Rinse and dry the boned breasts with paper towels. Pour the ginger ale into a quart-sized resealable plastic bag. Dump the breasts in and massage the bag a bit to get everything well mixed.
2. Place the bag in the refrigerator for 3 or 4 days, turning it morning and evening to keep all the pieces of meat well mixed in ginger ale.

COOKING

1. Preheat your barbecue to medium-high, about 600°F at cooking level. Drain the ginger ale off the breasts. Dry the breasts with paper towels and cut them into 6 to 8 bite-sized chunks. Cut the pepper and onion into equal-sized chunks.
2. Arrange the bacon on 8 skewers with the chunks of sharptail, peppers, and onions. Start each skewer by spearing one end of a strip of bacon and alternately spear pieces of sharptail and vegetables. End by wrapping the bacon around the kabob and spear it at the other end to secure it. Sprinkle with salt, pepper, and basil.
3. Place each kabob on the grill, cooking 8–10 minutes total and turning 3–4 times as they cook. Douse fat fires with a water pistol as necessary so the fat flare-ups don't burn your dinner.
4. When the bacon is done, so is everything else. Gently push the grilled meat and vegetables off each skewer onto a plate and serve with corn on the cob. ✸

Portly Sharptail Breasts

serves 4–6

Ingredients

2 teaspoons olive oil
2 teaspoons sugar
¼ cup minced shallots
3 cloves garlic, minced
1 teaspoon salt
½ teaspoon coarsely ground black pepper
⅔ cup port wine
3 teaspoons chicken bouillon granules
2 cups hot water
Boned breasts of 6 to 8 sharptails (or prairie chickens)

Next time you get lucky with sharptails, stop at the local bar on your way home and ask for ⅔ cup of port wine. That way you can try this moist, rich, tangy dish with little risk. My guess is that you'll start stocking port, and also start looking for those sharptail coveys just a bit harder.

COOKING

1. Preheat the oven to 325°F. In a 9- to 10-inch covered sauté pan (or Dutch oven) heat the oil and sugar over medium-high heat. When the oil starts to smoke, back the heat down to medium and add the shallots, garlic, salt, and pepper. Sauté until the shallots start to turn golden brown, stirring constantly, about 1 minute.

2. Add the port wine and stir it into the shallots. Continue sautéing over medium heat, stirring often, until the port wine has been reduced to about ⅓. (It will look thick, and feel slightly sticky on the spoon.) Combine the bouillon granules and water, and then add to the pan, stirring it into the thickened port wine.

3. As the pan comes back to a simmer, dry the sharptail breasts with paper towels, then bury them into the simmering pan juices. Cover the pan, and place it in the center of the oven. Continue cooking for another 45 minutes. Serve with egg noodles. ⊛

Fresh-Roasted Sharptails

Ingredients

*1 whole sharp-tailed grouse (or prairie chicken),
  plucked and cleaned*
¼ cup red currant jelly
*½ cup dry white wine (a dry Riesling—without
  too much oak—is good)*
1 tablespoon butter

I think the only thing more plentiful than game bird recipes are theories about game bird recipes. Wildlife photographer Bill Buckley has one about sharptails—namely, that they taste better when aged, plucked, and cooked without ever being frozen. This is the best way he's found to cook these never-frozen birds of the western prairies. If you're tolerant of medium-gamy flavor, you can try it with frozen birds.

COOKING

1. Preheat the oven to 325°F. Place the bird, breast side up, in an open roasting pan.
2. In a small bowl, melt the jelly in the microwave (about 30 seconds on high/700 watts) or in a saucepan over low heat until the jelly is liquefied. Combine the jelly with the white wine and pour over the bird. Rub the breast with the butter.
3. Place the roaster in the center of the oven. Roast the bird uncovered until medium-rare (55–60 minutes), basting often (at least 4–5 times) during the cooking. Remove the bird from the oven, let it sit 5–10 minutes, and carve, pouring the pan juices over the sliced meat.
4. Serve with buttered Brussels sprouts and buttermilk biscuits. ✸

Braised Sharptails

serves 4

Ingredients

2 sharptails (or prairie chickens), split
2 strips bacon, chopped
1 medium yellow onion, thickly sliced
2 teaspoons chicken bouillon granules
1¼ cups hot water
¼ teaspoon celery salt
½ teaspoon coarsely ground black pepper
⅛ teaspoon cayenne pepper

Braising (cooking in a small amount of liquid) is a great way to infuse naturally lean wild birds with moisture. This is one of my favorites for flavor. Use split birds so each person gets a leg and a breast, either plucked or skinned. If there are kids at the table, bone out the breasts and separate the legs from the carcass at the hip. That way you'll only have 3 large leg bones to worry about, and they're large enough to see easily. We don't have kids at home anymore, plus we love to eat birds with our fingers, so we tend to split the birds (see pages 167–169 for instructions).

COOKING

1. Rinse and dry the birds, trim any rough edges, and set aside.
2. Preheat the oven to 325°F. In a 10-inch skillet, sauté the bacon over medium heat until it starts to brown. Add the onions and continue over medium heat until the onions are soft, about 5 minutes for both.
3. Bury the 4 sharptail halves in the onions, and let them brown 1–2 minutes. In the meantime, combine the chicken bouillon granules, water, celery salt, black pepper, and cayenne pepper in a small bowl. Pour over the sharptails.
4. Raise the heat to high, and cook until the bouillon comes to a simmer. Transfer to the oven and cook for 1 hour. Serve hot with mashed potatoes. ◉

Slow-Cooked Sharptail Pockets

serves 2

Ingredients

1 cup beef bouillon
2 tablespoons Worcestershire sauce
1 tablespoon apple jelly, liquefied
1 tablespoon cherry preserves, liquefied
1 teaspoon onion powder
½ teaspoon dried leaf oregano
1 whole sharptail grouse (or prairie chicken)

Foil pockets are the hunter's answer to fussing with too-dry birds. This recipe keeps them moist and it's foolproof.

COOKING

1. Preheat the oven to 200°F. In a medium-sized bowl, combine the bouillon, Worcestershire sauce, apple jelly, cherry preserves, onion powder, and oregano. Stir to mix well.

2. Cut 3 lengths of foil, about 24 inches each. Using a loaf pan, place one piece of foil lengthwise, and press it into the loaf pan. Press the second piece of foil crosswise into the loaf pan. Leave the ends up to form a "boat" to hold the sauce.

3. Pour about ¼ of the sauce into the boat you've formed. Nestle the bird into the boat, and pour the rest of the sauce over the top. Seal each of the two layers, making it as watertight as possible. Then wrap the package in the third piece of foil and slip it back into the loaf pan. (The loaf pan will act as a drip catcher, if necessary.)

4. Place the loaf pan in the center of the oven and let it slow-cook for 8 hours, carefully turning the package 3 times (breast up to back up to breast up) during the cooking. Remove the bird from the "boat," and let cool about 5 minutes. Cut the legs and breast off, arrange on a platter, and pour the cooking sauce over the bird. Serve with hot German potato salad and peas. ☉

Maple-Smoked Sharptails

for 2 birds

Ingredients

2 cups hot water
½ cup non-iodized salt
⅓ cup plus 2 tablespoons maple syrup, in all
1 teaspoon dried orange peel
1 star anise, crushed
2 cups cold water
2 whole sharptails (or prairie chickens)
3 cups maple chips

I'm not fond of those smoked birds that resemble a hockey puck more than they resemble food. I like a smoked bird to be moist, tender, and delicious, and I'm referring to the thighs and drumsticks as much as the breast. This two-step approach is the best way I've found to accomplish this.

PREPARATION

1. In a 1-quart jar, combine the hot water, non-iodized salt, ⅓ cup of the maple syrup, all the orange peel, and the crushed star anise. Close the jar tightly and shake well. Let sit on the counter, shaking occasionally, until the salt dissolves. Add the 2 cups of cold water.
2. Pour this brine into a noncorrosive bowl or a resealable plastic bag large enough for the two birds.
3. Prepare the birds by trimming any rough edges and drying them thoroughly inside and out with paper towels. Place the birds in the brine. Cover the bowl, marinate in the refrigerator overnight (at least 12 hours).

SMOKING

1. Preheat your dry smoker to about 145°F and set 1 cup of maple chips into the smoker pan. Meanwhile, remove the birds from the brine and dry with paper towels. When the smoke begins

to emerge from the top, place the birds in the smoker.

2. Set a timer for 30 minutes and place another cup of chips into the wood pan. After 30 minutes, when the smoker quits smoking, add the last cup of chips. Sit back and relax.

3. After 3 hours of smoking, remove the birds from the smoker, wrap in foil, and cook for about 1 hour at 300°F in the oven. This will finish cooking the birds without drying them out. Serve hot, fresh from the oven, or chill overnight in the refrigerator. Serve on crackers with Cheddar cheese. ✸

Deli-Cured Sharptails

for 2 birds

Ingredients

2 tablespoons Morton's Tender Quick
1 teaspoon whole peppercorns
1 teaspoon whole mustard seeds
2 sharp-tailed grouse (or prairie chickens)
3 cups apple chips

Not only is this method of curing a bit neater than the brine method used in the Maple-Smoked Sharptails recipe, but it pushes the flavor of these little sharptails into the "pastrami" column. That's what pastrami is anyway: meat that's first salted, then smoked. And don't be surprised when the meat comes out bright red. It's done. It's just the salt cure talking.

PREPARATION

1. Combine the Tender Quick, peppercorns, and mustard seeds in a mortar and crush the whole spices coarsely. (Or place in a plastic bag and crush them with a rolling pin, wine bottle, or meat mallet.)
2. Prepare the grouse by trimming away any rough edges and fat, and drying inside and out with paper towels.
3. Divide the spice mix in half, and rub each bird all over inside and out with the mixture. Place the birds in a plastic bag, and let sit 6–8 hours in the refrigerator.

SMOKING

1. Preheat your dry smoker to about 145°F. (A Little Chief Smoker works automatically at that temperature.) Rinse the birds well, and dry with paper towels inside and out. Let sit at room temperature for 30 minutes while the smoker heats up.

2. Start 1 cup of the apple chips, and when you see smoke come out the top, place the birds into the smoker.

3. Set your timer for 30 minutes, and place another cup of chips into the wood pan. In another 30 minutes, when the smoker quits smoking, add the last cup of chips. Now, let the smoker work.

4. After 3 hours of smoking, remove the birds from the smoker, wrap in foil and cook for about 1 hour at 300°F in your oven. This will finish cooking the birds without drying them out. Serve hot, fresh from the oven, or chill overnight in the refrigerator and serve with a honey mustard salad dressing for dipping sauce. ✹

Quick Sharptail Hot Pot

serves 4

Ingredients

¼ cup chopped celery
¼ cup chopped onion
½ cup chopped red bell pepper
2 tablespoons oil
1 cup smoked sharptail (or prairie chicken) meat, shredded
1 cup cooked rice
1 cup canned black beans
1½ teaspoon garlic powder
1 teaspoon green pepper Tabasco sauce

Sure, you can eat your smoked birds on a cracker or mix them in scrambled eggs, but what do you do with the tiny, tidbits that are left over? Here's a quick dish you can fix for a tasty hot lunch that's guaranteed to stick to your ribs.

COOKING

1. In a large skillet, sauté the celery, onion, and red bell pepper in oil over medium heat until they begin to brown slightly.
2. Add the smoked meat, rice, black beans, garlic powder, and green Tabasco sauce. Stir to mix well and cook over medium heat until everything is hot. Serve with tortilla chips. ⊛

Sage Grouse Stroganoff

serves 4

Ingredients

3 tablespoons oil
2 medium yellow onions, sliced thin
2 cups sliced mushrooms
Boned breast of 1 sage grouse, sliced thin, across the grain
2 cups inexpensive brut champagne
½ cup sour cream
4 teaspoons beef bouillon granules (no water)
1 teaspoon salt
½ teaspoon pepper
¼ teaspoon nutmeg

No other bird is as easily adapted to this dish as sage grouse. Sage grouse have a dark, rich meat, and lots of it. Even a young bird will have 12–16 ounces of meat on the breast. And if you're worried about the "strong" prairie flavor, don't. Sour cream (as well as sweet cream) is an age-old ingredient in taming wild bird flavor.

COOKING

1. In a 9–10 inch covered skillet, heat the oil over medium heat, and sauté the onions and mushrooms until the onions just start to brown. Add the thinly sliced sage grouse meat, and stir it into the onions. Cook about 1–2 minutes, just to give the meat some color. Pour the champagne into the skillet, and let it come back to a simmer.

2. To the sour cream, add the beef bouillon granules, salt, pepper, and nutmeg. Stir to mix. When the skillet is simmering again, add the seasoned sour cream, and stir it into the onions. Bring the skillet back to a simmer, reduce the heat to low and cover it. Simmer about 30 minutes, until the meat is tender. Serve immediately over hot egg noodles or rice. ❀

Tip

Traditionally Stroganoff is made with white wine, but in many areas it's hard to find a white wine that has not been aged in oak, and oak is not a flavor you want to add to sage grouse. It's already got its own flavor, thank you very much. So I compromise: I buy inexpensive champagne and I make sure it's designated "brut" rather than "sec." That way I'm sure to have a nice dry white "wine" without oak to cook a good stroganoff. The good news is that the brut is also less expensive than those oaky whites.

Creamy Sage Grouse

serves 4

Ingredients

Boned breast of 1 sage grouse
2 tablespoons oil
1 tablespoon brown sugar
1 cup sliced onion
½ cup medium dry sherry
1½ teaspoons chicken bouillon granules
1 cup water
½ cup cream

A dish for sage breasts, or even a whole sharptail, separated into legs and breasts, with a rich sauce that goes well over rice, pasta, or toast. What a way to end a cold November day.

COOKING

1. Preheat the oven to 300°F. Cut each half of the sage breast into 2 to 3 pieces, across the grain, for easier handling. In an 8–9 inch covered skillet, heat the oil over medium heat, add the brown sugar, then lightly brown the sage breast pieces on both sides.
2. Add the onion, and dredge it in the pan juices. Combine the sherry with the bouillon granules, stir well, and when the onions are hot, add the sherry to the grouse. Let the sherry come to a simmer, then add the water and let it come to a simmer again. Add the cream and cover the skillet tightly.
3. Transfer the skillet to the oven, and let it cook about 2 hours. Serve over rice with garlic toast on the side. ◉

Sage Grouse Swiss Steak

serves 4

Ingredients

Boned breast of 1 sage grouse
2 cups buttermilk
¼ cup flour
2 teaspoons salt, in all
½ teaspoon pepper, in all
3 tablespoons oil
1 yellow onion, sliced
1 clove garlic, minced
2 stalks celery, chopped
1 28-ounce can diced tomatoes
1 cup beef bouillon
1 tablespoon Worcestershire sauce

Use a mature bird for this recipe if you like, then be sure to marinate it in the buttermilk overnight. Between that, the tenderizing, and the simmering, that old bird will melt in your mouth.

PREPARATION

1. The night before, trim and rinse the boned breasts. Pat dry with paper towels. Place in a bowl or resealable bag, and pour the buttermilk over. Place in the refrigerator overnight, turning once or twice.
2. When you're ready to cook, pour off the buttermilk and discard. Rinse the breast meat and pat dry. Set it aside.

COOKING

1. In a small bowl, combine the flour and 1 teaspoon of the salt with ¼ teaspoon of the pepper. Stir.
2. Sprinkle a bit of the seasoned flour on a cutting board, then pound both sides of the breast with a tenderizing mallet or the side of a plate as you sprinkle them with more of the seasoned flour. The breast halves should be quite thin. Cut them into serving-sized portions.
3. In a 9–10 inch covered skillet, heat the oil over medium heat, then lightly brown the floured breast pieces, about 2–3 minutes per side. Add the onion, garlic, celery, tomatoes, beef bouillon, the rest of the salt and pepper, and the Worcestershire sauce.
4. Bring the skillet to a low simmer, reduce the heat to low, and cover it. Let the breasts simmer about one hour, until the meat it quite tender. Serve with mashed potatoes and green beans. ❀

UPLAND GAME BIRD COOKERY

Mr. Fix-It Twice Cooked Sage Grouse

Ingredients

1 pound boned sage grouse breast
Cold water to cover
1 tablespoon commercial pickling spice
   or 1 teaspoon Cajun seasoning mix
2 eggs, lightly beaten
1 cup bread crumbs
4 tablespoons oil

Don't limit this recipe to sage grouse. It's a good way to cook any bird you have in your game bag, especially if it's tough or gamy.

PREPARATION

1. In a saucepan just large enough to fit the meat in a single layer, place the boned breasts and cover with water. Sprinkle the pickling spice over all. Cover and bring to a low boil. In the first few minutes, the breasts will plump up. Add more water, if necessary, to keep them just covered, then bring back to a low boil.
2. Cook for 60 minutes. The meat is ready when it's tender enough to stick a fork in. Pour off the seasoned water, and let the breasts cool to room temperature.

COOKING

1. Slice the breasts ¼-inch thick across the grain. Dredge first in the egg, then in the flour.
2. Heat the oil in a skillet over medium-high. Add the sliced breasts and cook about 3 minutes a side until the bread crumb coating is golden brown. Serve with hot German potato salad. ◉

Woodcock Want-Nots

Ingredients

2 wooden skewers for each bird
Breasts of several woodcock
1 water chestnut for each half breast
⅓ slice bacon for each wrap

Here's a recipe that fits right into the hurly-burly of hunting camp. Doesn't matter if you have one bird or four, as long as you have a can of water chestnuts around and a little bacon, you can make a quick appetizer to tide you over until dinner's ready. Notice that even non-cooks can do this one. But please don't overcook the woodcock: they're delicious when slightly pink. Well done and they'll develop a "livery" flavor.

COOKING

1. Soak the skewers for 30 minutes in cold water. Bone the breast meat from the woodcock, saving the tenderloin for Caesar Salad à la Woodcock (see page 102) tomorrow night if you want. Lay each breast half on the cutting board and, with the palm of your hand, press it flat, and just a bit longer, so it will wrap around the chestnut. Then wrap that with ⅓ slice of bacon, and run a skewer through the thickest part.

2. Preheat the grill to medium heat. When the grill is ready, pop the bacon-wrapped breasts on the grill and cook about 5–8 minutes, turning often, until the breasts are still pink in the middle and the bacon is browned. Serve immediately, either alone or with chips and dip. ✽

Grilled Woodcock with Jack Daniels Barbecue Sauce

serves 2–4

Ingredients

4–8 woodcock, plucked and split
1 quart buttermilk

FOR THE SAUCE

¼ cup oil
2 cups diced onion
2 tablespoons minced garlic
1 cup Jack Daniels
1 cup ketchup
½ cup brown sugar
4 tablespoons Worcestershire sauce
2 teaspoons prepared bacon bits

The trick to grilling woodcock is to do it until there is just a little pink left and the meat is still moist. Aside from that, the buttermilk does the work, mellowing out the dark meat taste—these are dark-breasted birds after all—and tenderizing it at the same time. And be careful of those legs. Tuck the knees in against the body each time you turn them. Those legs aren't dark meat at all. They're pale and delicious. (Unlike sage and sharp-tailed grouse, which are dark all over, woodcock apparently don't walk much. Thus white legs—and plump and meaty drumsticks.)

PREPARATION

1. Remove the backbones (see details on page 167). Wipe dry inside and out with paper towels. Marinate the woodcock overnight in the buttermilk.
2. In a saucepan, heat the oil over medium heat, add the onions and garlic and sauté until soft, about 4–5 minutes. Add the bourbon, ketchup, brown sugar, Worcestershire, and bacon bits, and stir well. Bring the pan to a simmer, and lower the heat to low. Simmer about 10 minutes until the bourbon flavor has mellowed. (You're actually cooking the alcohol out, leaving only the rich flavor.) Cool, then refrigerate until ready to use.

COOKING

1. Pour half of the barbecue sauce into a small bowl. Save the rest for the table. Preheat the barbecue to medium, about 400°F. Drain the buttermilk from the woodcock and discard it. Rinse and dry the woodcock inside and out with paper towels.
2. When the barbecue is ready, lightly oil the skin on each bird, and place on the grill. Spoon some of the barbecue sauce on each bird. Cover the grill, and cook about 15 minutes total time, turning the birds and basting them with the barbecue sauce every 3 minutes. (They should be turned at least 4 times, and they should be done when there's just a little pink left.)
3. Remove the birds from the grill, and serve hot with the rest of the barbecue sauce for dipping.

Caesar Salad à la Woodcock

serves 4

Ingredients

½ cup olive oil
2 cloves garlic
1 head romaine lettuce, in chunks
3 tablespoons red wine vinegar
½ teaspoon dry mustard
1 teaspoon salt
⅛ teaspoon black pepper
1 tablespoon egg substitute
6–8 drops Worcestershire sauce
1 cup cubed French bread
Tenderloins of 8–10 woodcock
1 tablespoon grated Parmesan cheese

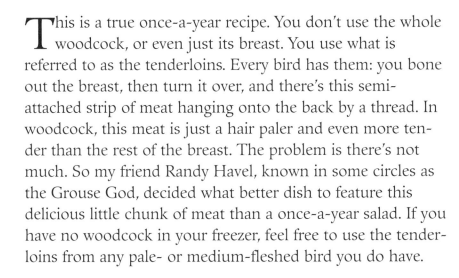

This is a true once-a-year recipe. You don't use the whole woodcock, or even just its breast. You use what is referred to as the tenderloins. Every bird has them: you bone out the breast, then turn it over, and there's this semi-attached strip of meat hanging onto the back by a thread. In woodcock, this meat is just a hair paler and even more tender than the rest of the breast. The problem is there's not much. So my friend Randy Havel, known in some circles as the Grouse God, decided what better dish to feature this delicious little chunk of meat than a once-a-year salad. If you have no woodcock in your freezer, feel free to use the tenderloins from any pale- or medium-fleshed bird you do have.

PREPARATION

About 10 days in advance, pour the oil in a jar, cut the garlic cloves in half, and drop them in, too. Cover and refrigerate until ready to use.

COOKING

1. Arrange the romaine lettuce in 4 bowls. In a small bowl, combine 6 tablespoons of the garlic oil, all the red wine vinegar, mustard, salt, pepper, egg substitute, and Worcestershire sauce. Stir to dissolve the mustard, and mix the liquids thoroughly. Set aside.

2. In a small skillet, sauté the cubed French bread in 2 tablespoons of the garlic oil until the bread cubes start to brown. Remove from the pan, and let the croutons cool.
3. In the same pan, heat 1 more tablespoon of the garlic oil over medium heat, then add the tenderloins, and sauté until the tenderloins are just cooked, about 2–3 minutes.
4. To assemble the salad: Stir up the dressing, then spoon about half of it over the lettuce. Arrange the croutons and (still warm) tenderloins over the lettuce, sprinkle with Parmesan cheese, and serve immediately, with the rest of the dressing at the table. ✸

Camp Cook's Favorite Woodcock

Ingredients

2–3 whole birds per person
Enough club soda to cover the birds
3 slices bacon, diced
1 large yellow onion, sliced
1 cup flour
1 teaspoon garlic salt
1 teaspoon salt
1 teaspoon pepper

From my favorite woodcock-ruffed grouse camp in Michigan, the favorite recipe of the camp cook. And since this camp cook also hunts, he knows all about luck, and filling up game vests. Thus this recipe is built like an expando-file: adaptable to both good days and bad. (Try to allow 2–3 birds per person.)

PREPARATION

1. Place the birds in a deep bowl or resealable plastic bag, and pour the club soda over them. Marinate overnight.
2. Drain off the club soda, and pull the meat off the bones. Let the meat come to room temperature before cooking.

COOKING

1. Over medium-high heat, cook the bacon and the onion in an 8- to 9-inch skillet until the bacon is browned. Remove the onion and bacon from the skillet, and set them aside and cover with foil to keep warm.
2. In a plastic bag, combine the flour, garlic salt, salt, and pepper. Toss the pulled meat in the seasoned flour.
3. On high heat, drop the pulled woodcock in the bacon grease, and sauté lightly until the birds are just pink, about 5–6 minutes. Look for blood to come through the flour (it may only make the flour pink), and they're ¾ done. Then turn and cook only 1 more minute. Throw the bacon and onions back in the skillet, and cook only 1 more minute. The camp cook warns, "Don't overcook these birds or dinner will be tough and livery." ❋

John's Ten Minute Soup

serves 4

Ingredients

4 cups chicken broth
4 ounces lightly smoked polish sausage, diced
4 ounces young sharptail, sage, or woodcock meat
   (½–¾ cup), diced
½ cup chopped yellow onion
1 tablespoon oil
1 15.5-ounce can of corn
½ teaspoon black pepper

My husband John is usually the lunch cook at our house, mostly because he gets his morning work done sooner than I do and can't wait around for me. So I often am torn away from my work by the tantalizing aroma of one of his delicious concoctions—like this. His lunch cooking is always fast but never simple in flavors. (The trick to this recipe's quickness is to use young, tender meat. Of any kind. The broth will add the moisture.)

COOKING

1. In a medium-sized sauce pan, bring the broth to a boil over high heat. Add the sausage and boned meat, and bring the pot back to a low boil. Turn down to a simmer, and let it cook while you sauté the onions.

2. In a medium-sized skillet, sauté the onion in the oil over medium heat until the onion turns slightly brown, about 5 minutes. Add the onion to the broth. Then add the corn and black pepper and let everything simmer about 5 minutes until the corn is hot. Serve immediately with toast. ❁

Hungry Hunter Dinner-In-A-Dish

serves 6–8

Ingredients

2 pounds diced dark-fleshed birds (about 5 cups)
3 tablespoons oil, in all
1 large yellow onion, sliced fairly thick
½ cup Marsala wine
2 cups beef bouillon
1 tablespoon bottled bacon bits
2 15-ounce cans stewed tomatoes
1½ teaspoons dried leaf thyme
½ teaspoon dried leaf basil
½ teaspoon garlic powder
½ teaspoon whole fennel seed
¾ cup uncooked rice

Use your darkest birds for this dish, tossing both boned breast and leg meat into the pot. That's the joy of soup: everything goes. And this soup goes anywhere. Fill a small thermos for a cold morning's hunt; it keeps you going longer than coffee and candy bars. Or pack the whole pot of soup to take camping. While one person sets up tents and sleeping bags, you can reheat this one-course meal on the camp stove.

COOKING

1. In a 5-quart Dutch oven, lightly brown the diced meat in the oil over medium-high heat. Work in batches, using about 1 tablespoon of oil per batch, and set each batch aside as you go. When the meat is done, sauté the onion until lightly brown, about 4 minutes.

2. As you finish, add the Marsala to the pan and stir up all the tasty bits from the bottom. Let the Marsala cook until the pan is almost dry again, about 4 minutes. Then add all the browned meat, beef bouillon, bottled bacon pieces, tomatoes, thyme, basil, garlic powder, and fennel and stir the pot well.

3. Bring the pot back to a simmer and add the uncooked rice. Stir well, cover, and simmer 1–2 hours until the meat is tender and the rice cooked.

4. Serve with hard rolls and butter. ◉

Chapter Six

Turkeys

There is no big mystery to good turkey cooking. As Bo Pitman, turkey guide extraordinaire, points out, you just have to "seal the 'ception in."

We were in the dining room at White Oak Plantation after a hard day's work when Bo started in on " 'ception." I didn't doubt him. In the last 12 hours, I'd seen him make one turkey walk three quarters of a mile uphill, and another forget he already had a hen. Both birds were now hanging in the cooler. I figured that anyone who can fool turkeys this well would know a trick or two about cooking them, too.

"Now wait a minute," I'd said. "What the heck is this 'ception?" And Bo seemed to start to explain, but like the Brahma bulls he used to ride, he's a little hard to pin down.

In the end, I decided, this 'ception Bo speaks of is a combination of things: from the natural juices of the bird to the hunter's own anticipation of how good it's going to taste. And the important part is to seal everything into the bird—whether you fry it, roast it, or simply grill it on the barbecue. I think Bo would include roasting bags, marinade injectors, and aluminum foil in the category of 'ception sealers.

As vague as he is about the meaning of 'ception, he is just as oppositely precise about the other crucial part of turkey cooking: "Don't overcook the durn thing! That 'ception's delicate."

Robert P's Quick Sautéed Turkey Breast

serves 2

Ingredients

1 pound boned turkey breast (2½–3 cups),
  in bite-sized pieces
½ teaspoon salt
¼ teaspoon white pepper
2 tablespoons butter
1 tablespoon fresh marjoram
1 tablespoon chopped chives
1 tablespoon chopped parsley

This may be the easiest recipe I've ever cooked, and one of the easiest to remember. If you don't have fresh marjoram, improvise with basil, sage, oregano, or tarragon. According to Robert Pittman, co-owner of White Oak Plantation, the important thing is to simply use fresh herbs and real butter. No substituting margarine for this dish, please.

COOKING

1. Dry the turkey bites with paper towels, and season with the salt and pepper.
2. Melt the butter gently in the pan over medium heat until it starts to sizzle. Add the turkey chunks, marjoram, chives, and parsley. Sauté the meat, stirring it as it cooks to make sure all sides of the chunks get cooked, about 4 to 5 minutes at most.
3. Arrange on a platter over rice or egg noodles and serve with fresh asparagus. ✺

White Oak Turkey Breast

serves 4

Ingredients

1 side of a mature turkey breast
2 teaspoons prepared Cajun seasoning mix

Calvin is the cook at White Oak Plantation, Tuskegee, Alabama, one of my favorite places to hunt, and eat southern style. While I freely admit I don't get grits, Calvin's favorite turkey recipe is hard to top. You'll need a nice day outdoors for this one and a deep fryer and frying basket with enough peanut or canola oil to cover the breast.

COOKING

1. Preheat the oil to 350°F in the deep fryer. Trim the breast, and dry with paper towels. Rub the Cajun seasoning mix all over the breast and place in the fryer basket.
2. When the oil is hot, slowly submerge the breast into the hot oil and cook about 8 minutes. Remove from the oil, drain on paper towels, and let cool.
3. Slice thick or thin across the grain, and serve with your own homemade French fries. ◉

Turkey Nuggets

serves 6–8

Ingredients

FOR THE COOL DIPPING SAUCE

¾ cup mayonnaise
½ cup prepared horseradish
2 tablespoons freshly squeezed lemon juice

FOR THE TANGY TOMATO-GARLIC DIPPING SAUCE

¼ cup sour cream
2 tablespoons sun-dried tomatoes (in oil)
2 cloves garlic
1 teaspoon minced mild jalapeño (from a can)
1 teaspoon chopped onion

FOR THE TURKEY

1 cup flour
2 eggs, lightly beaten
2 tablespoons water
1 cup corn flake crumbs
1 teaspoon salt
1 teaspoon sugar
½ teaspoon celery salt
½ teaspoon onion powder
½ teaspoon garlic powder
8 ounces turkey meat (1⅓ cups), in bite-sized chunks

Use turkey breast or dark, juicy chunks of thigh meat to create this great appetizer. Either way, cut away any connective tissue; these tender morsels cook up quickly. Do try both dips included here. One's cool and creamy; the other will blow your mind. Just what you need whether it's a hot summer day or cold winter night.

PREPARATION

1. In a small bowl, combine the mayonnaise, horseradish, and lemon juice. Stir. Cover tightly and refrigerate overnight.
2. In a small blender, purée together the sour cream, tomatoes, garlic, jalapeño, and onion. Transfer to a small bowl, cover tightly, and refrigerate overnight.

COOKING

1. Preheat a Fry Daddy to 375°F. In three bowls, set out the flour, the egg (beaten with the water), and the corn flake crumbs. To the corn flakes, add the salt, sugar, celery salt, onion powder, and garlic powder. Stir into the corn flakes.
2. When the oil is hot, start dredging the chunks of turkey: first in the flour, then the egg, then the corn flakes. Drop gently into the hot oil and let the chunks cook a few at a time until golden brown, about 2–3 minutes. Drain on paper towels.
3. Serve as an appetizer with the two dipping sauces.

Easy Cajun Turkey Breast

serves 4

Ingredients

2 tablespoons olive oil
1 medium onion, diced
½ green bell pepper, diced
2 cloves garlic, minced
1 teaspoon dried basil flakes
1 teaspoon dried thyme leaves
1 teaspoon sweet paprika
1 teaspoon salt
½ teaspoon white pepper
¼ teaspoon cayenne pepper
One side of a boned turkey breast (about 1½–2 pounds)

Richard Beebe, the engineering genius behind Redding reloading dies, is also a pretty good magician. How else can you explain his being able to make a gobbler fly over water, walk uphill, and—losing all good sense—jump up on a rock to show off his manly physique within 15 yards of a shotgun? Abracadabra, we had dinner.

COOKING

1. In a large skillet, heat the oil over medium-high heat and add the onion, bell pepper, and garlic. Lower the heat to medium and sauté until the onion is softened, about 3–4 minutes. Add the basil, thyme, paprika, salt, white pepper, and cayenne pepper, and stir to completely coat the vegetables. Sauté about 1 minute more and remove from heat. Let this mixture cool at room temperature.

2. Preheat your barbecue to 375° to 400°F for indirect cooking (see page 59 for details). Layer two 24-inch lengths of foil on a cookie sheet. Spread one third of the onion mixture on the back side of the breast and lay the breast (herb-side down) in the center of the foil. Spread the rest of the onion mixture on the top of the breast. Seal the foil package.

3. Place the cookie sheet on the grate away from the fire. Close the barbecue.

4. Cook for about 55–60 minutes, until a meat thermometer inserted in the thickest part of the breast registers 160°F. Cover the package again, bring it inside, and let it sit on the counter 10 minutes before carving. All pink will be gone, and the meat will be moist and delicious. Carve in thick slices and serve with Cajun-style rice.

5. Alternatives: On really hot days, you can cook this Cajun breast the night before, then chill overnight (still wrapped in the foil), and serve cold. On cold days, you can cook the package in your kitchen oven at 375°F. ✸

Turkey Chow Mein

Ingredients

1 cup chicken broth
1 tablespoon cornstarch
2 tablespoons soy sauce
1 teaspoon ground ginger
2 teaspoons sugar
½ teaspoon monosodium glutamate (MSG)
1 tablespoon oil
2 stalks celery, chopped
1 cup coarsely chopped onion
8 ounces boned turkey breast
1 14-ounce can bean sprouts, drained
1 8-ounce can bamboo shoots, drained and rinsed

Where I live, turkey hunting is a 2-bird-a-year proposition, if you're lucky. So I prefer to pluck the whole bird and roast it for a holiday dinner, where it will draw all the hoopla a wild turkey deserves. If your bird is damaged, however, or if you're lucky enough to have more birds than holidays, you probably have a lot of boned turkey meat in the freezer. Thaw out a little. Chow mein is a great way to keep that low-fat wild meat moist while you cook it. And it's a quick dish for busy weeknights.

COOKING

1. In a small bowl, combine the broth, cornstarch, soy sauce, ginger, sugar, and MSG. Stir and set aside.
2. In a large skillet or a wok, heat the oil over medium-high heat and sauté the celery and onion until it is just tender, about 4–5 minutes. Add the seasoned broth and stir until the mixture comes to a simmer. Add the turkey chunks, stirring them into the sauce until they are well coated. Once the sauce comes back up to a simmer, turn the heat down to medium and continue cooking (4–5 minutes total) until the turkey has turned opaque (white and not shiny-looking).
3. Add the bean sprouts and bamboo shoots and toss them with the rest of the ingredients. Continue cooking until the bean sprouts and bamboo shoots are hot. Serve immediately over fried Chinese noodles or rice. ✸

Tip

Good wok cooking is hot, hot, hot. Use oils with a high smoking point, like canola or peanut oil. Then wait until you see thin wisps of smoke swirling off the oil before you throw the food in.

The Un-Traditional Fourth of July Fried Turkey

serves 6–8

Ingredients

1 whole plucked jake turkey (see Tip)
Canola or peanut oil to cover the bird (see Tip)
Marinade injector
¾ cup pulpless orange juice
6 tablespoons butter, softened
2¼ teaspoons green pepper Tabasco sauce
1½ teaspoons ground cumin
¾ teaspoon garlic salt

Here's a meal for our favorite summer holiday that uses the same ingredients as our favorite winter holiday meal, but turns them on their ear. Start with a fried turkey that cooks in a record 3 minutes a pound; then use sweet potatoes instead of white ones for your potato salad; and finish with a garden salad tossed with dried cranberries. Please read all the safety precautions before using your fryer. And remember: It takes hours for the oil to cool down again. Have a safe Fourth of July.

Tip

Why canola or peanut oil? They both have a high enough smoking point to fry the turkey at 350°F without smoking. That's important because if the oil doesn't smoke, it's not burning and you can re-use it. To re-use oil, first strain it: Nestle a small metal sieve in a funnel as you transfer the cooled oil back into its original containers, or buy a pump-operated filter for recycling fryer oil. Toss the last 1 to 2 inches of used oil. Store the strained oil in a cool, dark place.

PREPARATION

1. Thoroughly thaw the turkey in the refrigerator (allow 4–5 days in the bottom of the refrigerator). Check for stray feathers, trim jagged edges, rinse with cold water inside and out, and dry with paper towels, again inside and out. Let the turkey sit at room temperature and air dry while you heat the oil and prepare the marinade.

2. Fill your fryer with enough oil to cover the bird. (See page 116 for details.) Attach the frying thermometer to the side of the pot, cover, and heat the oil to 350°F. (In moderate weather, about 40 minutes.)

3. In a small bowl, combine the orange juice, butter, green pepper sauce, cumin, and garlic salt. Stir by hand, or put these ingredients through the blender, to completely mix them. Fill the marinade injector syringe with about ¼ of the orange juice mixture, and inject it into one side of the breast. Repeat with the other side and both legs, spreading the marinade through the meat as shown in the injector directions. (You can also inject the marinade the night before, and let the juices work overnight on the chilled turkey.)

COOKING

1. When the oil is hot, place the bird on the cooking rack and lower it carefully into the oil to prevent burning yourself. (It also helps to wear elbow-length oven mitts—or welding gloves—and long, loose pants.) Cook no more than 3 minutes per pound at 350°F. The bird will be totally cooked, with no pink, in that hot oil.

2. Lift the cooking rack carefully, using the hook and a long oven mitt, and set the bird on paper towels to cool about 10 minutes before moving it indoors and carving it; it is going to drip very hot oil for a few minutes. Carve as you would your Christmas turkey.

3. Alternately, cook the bird the day before, chill it overnight in the refrigerator, and serve cold. It will be just as good, maybe better on a hot summer day.

4. For the alternative holiday meal, serve with sweet potato salad, green salad tossed with "craisins" (dried cranberries), and a little Gorgonzola cheese. Then prepare potato salad with 6 boiled sweet potatoes, 6 hard-boiled eggs, 1 cup each chopped onions, celery, mayonnaise, and a pinch of cinnamon. Salt and pepper taste. ◎

Tip

Be sure you "pre-fit" the turkey to the fryer pot. Weight guidelines are different for wild turkeys, since they are longer and narrower than commercially raised turkeys.

First, check the depth of the pot. My fryer is 16 inches deep, which is just enough to fry an 8-pound oven-ready jake. The long-beard turkey in my freezer was a good 4 inches longer and would not have fit without removing the thigh and drumstick and cooking them separately. So before you fill the pot up with oil, stick the turkey on the cooking rack (legs up), lower it into the empty pot, and make sure it fits.

Second, find out how much oil you'll need. While you've got the turkey in the empty pot, use an empty gallon jug to fill the pot with cold tap water until the bird is completely immersed. (You can do this job outdoors with the garden hose, but use a hose rated for drinking water.) The amount for each bird differs because fatter birds displace more oil, thinner birds—spring birds, for instance, which have things other than eating on their minds—displace less oil.

Now lift the turkey out, empty the pot, dry it out with paper towels, and set it in the sun to dry completely. You don't want any tiny droplets of water in the pot when you start adding oil.

Converting water to oil: For this 8-pound turkey, it took 6 gallons of cold water to cover the bird in my 16-inch tall, 12-inch inside-diameter pot. Then, since hot oil expands, deduct about 1 quart from that total.

UPLAND GAME BIRD COOKERY

Tipsy-Dipsy Roasted Turkey

serves 6–8

Ingredients

1 mature turkey, about 12 pounds oven-ready

FOR THE STUFFING
3 tablespoons butter
¼ cup cognac (or 1 50-ml airline-sized bottle)
1 golden delicious apple, cored and diced
1 nectarine, pitted and diced
¼ cup almonds, chopped coarsely

FOR THE PAN JUICES
¼ cup cold water
3 tablespoons cornstarch

I think Bo Pitman would approve of this recipe because it triples up on 'ception savers (see introduction to this chapter). An oven bag is paired with moist dressing and the whole bird is cooked upside down to make sure the juices flow into the breast meat and not out of it. The 12-pound bird in this recipe was an 18-pound, 3-year-old tom on the hoof. If your bird varies by a few pounds, just allow about 12 minutes per pound for a lightly stuffed bird. Turkeys cook faster in the oven bag, so you don't need the usual 15 minutes per pound. These big toms have an ugly fat pad that lies between the craw and the breast. It doesn't affect flavor, but when you carve the breast meat, slice it off before placing the meat on a platter.

COOKING

1. Rinse and dry the turkey inside and out with paper towels. Set it aside.
2. In a medium-sized skillet, heat the butter over medium-high heat until it starts to sizzle. Add the cognac, let it sizzle 20 or 30 seconds. Stir in the chopped apple, nectarine, and almonds. Stir until the fruit and nuts are well coated. Continue cooking about 2–3 minutes all together until the fruit just starts to soften. Remove from the heat and let that sit.

3. Preheat the oven to 350°F. Prepare a turkey-sized plastic oven bag according to package directions (including dusting it with 1 tablespoon of flour and cutting six ½-inch slits in the top of the bag). Place the turkey in the bag and set the bag (with the turkey breast-side down) on a poultry rack set in a roasting pan. Spoon the stuffing into the bird.

4. Close the bag and place the roaster, uncovered, in the center of the oven. Let the bird cook 2½ hours. Then cut open the top of the bag and check the internal temperature with a meat thermometer. It should read 160°F.

5. Carefully remove the turkey from the bag and let it sit 10 minutes on a cutting board for easier slicing. In the meantime, pour the pan juices through a sieve into a saucepan. Add the water and cornstarch. You should have about 3 cups of pan juices; if not, reduce the corn starch, allowing one tablespoon per 1 cup of pan juices. Stir constantly over medium-high heat until the pan juices come to a low boil and thicken up.

6. Carve the turkey as you would a commercial one, removing the legs first at the hip, and then slicing the breast meat off thick or thin, depending on how your family likes it. Serve with the thickened pan juices. ⊛

Leftover Gobblin' Hoppin' John

serves 4

Ingredients

1 cup rice
4 cups chicken broth, in all
2 slices bacon, coarsely chopped
1 cup chopped onion
½ cup chopped green bell pepper
1 clove garlic, minced
3 cups diced cooked turkey
1 15-ounce can black-eyed peas, rinsed and drained
1 teaspoon salt
2 bay leaves

John and I have been making Hoppin' John on New Year's Day for years. It started when we lived in a tiny town in central Montana where the only bar in town was owned by a woman of incredible energy and warmth, who was never at a loss for good advice. Meredith informed us that if we ever wanted to have good luck in our lives, we must start each year with black-eyed peas, and the best way to eat black-eyed peas, she told us, was Hoppin' John. Meredith is now dishing out advice to the angels, but we still make Hoppin' John on New Year's Day. This year, we made our good luck with the leftover tidbits from a 20-pound Merriam's turkey we'd roasted for Christmas. If you don't have any leftover cooked meat, use any boned turkey meat, legs or breast, and add it with the broth in Step 2 just the same.

PREPARATION

Cook the rice in 2 cups of the broth: Add the rice to boiling broth, and once the pot returns to a low boil, turn the heat as low as it will go, stir the rice once, and cover the pot. Cook 15–20 minutes, without looking, until the rice has "eyes" and all the broth has been absorbed.
Set aside.

COOKING

1. In a 3-quart Dutch oven, sauté the bacon over medium-high heat until

light brown. Add the onion, green pepper, and garlic to the pan, and sauté until they are tender, about 4–5 minutes.

2. Add the turkey, black-eyed peas, salt, bay leaf, and the rest of the chicken broth. Stir to combine and bring back to a low simmer. Cover the pot, reduce the heat to low, and cook until all the liquid has been absorbed, about 40–50 minutes.

3. Remove the bay leaves, stir the rice into the Hoppin' John, and simmer another 5–10 minutes until the rice is hot. Serve immediately.

Tip

If you'd rather use dried black-eyed peas instead of canned, start them the night before. Rinse 1 cup of dried peas in cold water. Bring 5 cups of water to a rolling boil. Add the peas and bring the pot back to a medium rolling boil. Boil 2 minutes, remove from the heat, and let them sit, covered, overnight. Rinse and drain thoroughly and use as you would the canned beans. That should measure about two cups, same as the can.

UPLAND GAME BIRD COOKERY

Chapter Seven

Sausages and Smoking

Now's the time to pull out all those birds you've been neglecting in your freezer and make them into delicious sausage. Dig deep. Any bird that's freezer burned or that is simply too gamy for your family's tastes will make great sausage. Trust me. I've been doing this for years, and there's nothing so exciting as bringing a plateful of bratwurst to the table and having your family and guests devour them. You don't have to tell them what they're eating—unless you want to brag.

But before you get started, here are a few basic guidelines. First, cleanliness—and refrigeration—are next to Godliness. Second, two pairs of hands are better than one—especially if this is the first time you've cased sausage. And third, never, never, never taste raw sausage mix.

Cleanliness—And Refrigeration—Are Next to Godliness

It seems I'm always making sausage with the leftover birds from the last hunting season. Which means it's August and almost time to start again. According to the experts, the ideal time to make sausage is when the weather is cool. In real life, the ideal time is whenever you can make the time. With sausage that just means you pay a little more attention to keeping the sausage mix cool.

Why is temperature so important? First, keeping the meat cool, even slightly frozen, means that it's somewhat stiff when it hits the working end of the grinder and less of the meat's natural juices are released. That makes for more moist and flavorful sausage. Second, all meat, commercial or wild, has bacteria. Freezing stops growth. Thawing starts the process again, and the longer any meat is left above 32°F, the more opportunity those bacteria have to multiply and prosper. How warm is your kitchen in August? In December? In a modern home the indoor temperature rarely falls below 65°F. Plenty of opportunity for healthy little germs.

Follow the well-known rules for meat handling. Clean all cutting, grinding, and counter surfaces with hot, soapy water. Wash hands between tasks (like grinding meat and picking up the phone or a sandwich). Always keep the pork, beef suet, chicken, and game meats cool when processing sausage. In practice:

1. Don't leave meat out on the counter to defrost. Do it in the refrigerator or in short 1–2 minute bursts on the defrost setting in the microwave. Check the meat for warm spots between bursts, and then limit total time, bursts and resting, to 30–40 minutes. In order to reserve as much as the meat's moisture as possible, don't even thaw the cuts completely; just enough to safely cut strips that easily fit into your grinder.

2. Return all meat to the refrigerator between steps, even if there's a pause of only a few minutes.

3. Once the grinding, mixing, and casing are done, either cook or refrigerate the sausages immediately. If you intend to freeze a batch of sausage for later, double wrap (cased or uncased) pressing all the air out of the packages very diligently. Then plan to store them for no more than 3–4 months. Fat is more susceptible to freezer burn than muscle (which is what lean meat is), and ground meat has much more surface area to be exposed to the cold dry air of the freezer— thus increasing its tendency to freezer burn.

4. When you take the sausages back out of the freezer to cook, go back to the first point: thaw in the refrigerator or short bursts in the microwave (and remember that fat cooks faster in a microwave, so fat-added sausage will thaw much faster than lean meat alone). Don't thaw meat on the counter.

Two Pairs of Hands Are Better Than One

The choice of whether or not you case sausage is often simply a matter of how many hands you have available. And for some fresh sausages—like the Traditional Sage Breakfast Sausage, Fresh-Mex Breakfast Sausage, and Italian Garden Sausage—patties are just as easy to cook and certainly easier to make. The other sausages in this book, though, are simply not sausages unless they're cased. Casing sausages alone—while filling the grinder with mix and keeping it at an even pressure so as not to burst the casings or create air pockets—is a daunting task.

The question is: How many hands can you muster? At our house there are four hands, belonging to my husband and myself. My husband feeds the grinder while I handle the stuffed casings coming out the other end. If I had four more hands, one pair would be boning the birds for the next batch, while the other pair would be double wrapping, labeling, and toting the first finished sausages to the freezer.

Never, Never, Never Taste Raw Sausage

You'll notice in most of these recipes there are instructions to let the sausage mix sit overnight before you case, freeze, or cook it. This is to let the flavors in the spices develop fully before the process is cut off. But how do you know when you have the right combination? You need to taste it—once before it sits overnight, to make sure you're close, and a final taste after it has rested overnight.

To taste safely, the sausage mix must be cooked. The easiest way I've found to do that is to place a teaspoon-sized ball of the sausage mixture in a tea cup and cook it in the microwave on high until the pink is all gone (about 1 minute at 700 watts, which is high on my old machine). While cooking it in the microwave tends to make the sausage tough, it is a perfectly good way to test for salt, pepper, and other seasonings, and using a 2-inch-deep tea cup (as opposed to a flat saucer) keeps cleanup to a minimum.

For those without microwaves, take the same teaspoon-sized ball of sausage and quickly fry it in a bit of oil on medium heat in a skillet. After 3 or 4 minutes cut the ball in half, making sure it has no pink inside, then cool it a bit and pop it in your mouth. Some people like more salt, some less.

If your first response is that the sausage needs more heat, hang on for 24 hours. Heat grows. Peppers, ginger, coriander—any spice that adds heat—should only be augmented after the mix has had a chance to develop for 24 hours.

So keep your mix cool, call your friends for help (have them bring their birds over, too), and never—no matter how delicious it looks—put the tiniest bit of raw mix in your mouth. Now all you have to do is decide whether to case the sausage or not.

How Much Fat is Enough ?

Sausage, by nature, is a fatty meat. Since game birds have very little to no fat, you must add pork fat, chicken, or beef suet to give your wursts their best flavor and texture. A ratio of about 25–35 percent fat is best. While I always favor the leaner side of that percentage, the sausages that taste the best are, truthfully, the ones that tip over toward the fat side. When you are making your own sausage, there's no fighting this. Make your sausages too lean, and they'll be dry and unappetizing. If you worry about fat, just accept that once in a while you need to splurge. Use moderation in eating—not mixing—your dogs, brats, and wursts, and take pleasure in having total control of their contents.

To Case Or Not To Case

If you don't own an electric grinder yet, now is a good time to spend the $100 for one. Most grinders come with at least one stuffing tube, and that is by far the easiest way to stuff sausage.

As for casings, hog casings, which fill into the typical bratwurst-sized sausages, are the most commonly available. They come frozen or packed in salt, with directions on the back of the package for preparing the casings and stuffing the sausage.

Beyond that, you need to know: oiling the outside of the stuffing tube makes loading the casings lots easier; soaking more than the recommended 1 foot of casing per 1 pound of sausage mix is simply a case of realizing that time is money; and following the last bit of sausage with a couple of slices of torn up bread will not only help you get more of the sausage out of the grinder and into the casing, but will scour the insides of the grinder and make cleanup easier.

If you get into sausage making, you may want to try lamb-sized synthetic casings that will provide the more typical thin breakfast links. The casings can often be found in butcher shops that make their own sausage and in sausage-making catalogs. Lamb casings need the smaller stuffing tube, available in the same sausage-making catalogs, though sometimes a grinder will come with both hog-sized and lamb-sized stuffing tubes. Look for a grinder that has all-metal moving parts: the augur, the cutting blade, and any other moving parts around the augur. Plastic will break down and not be worth your money, no matter how little you paid.

Invest In Spices

Some of these recipes call for fresh herbs: basil, thyme, sage, and the like. If they're not available fresh, you can often substitute dried leaf herbs, simply using half of the quantity called for in the recipe. This works well for spices and fairly well for most herbs, but it does not work well at all for dried cilantro and parsley, which resemble last year's baled hay more than their fresh counterpart. The good news, of course, is that parsley—and lately cilantro—are widely available. I also grow a few of my favorite herbs, which is another reason I'm generally making sausage in August; I'm usually knee-deep in thyme.

When dried herbs and spices are called for, do yourself a flavor favor and splurge on new spices for the project. Why? Insurance. Even the most carefully stored chili powder, red pepper flakes, and ginger loses potency when kept several months in the spice closet. (And who knows how long it was on the shelf at the store before you took it home.) Manufacturers recommend only 3–6 months storage before replacement. While that is a bit extravagant for everyday cooking, making sausage takes a little time, and it's worth a few bucks to ensure great results.

Just a Little Off the Top

That's what trimming is. Whether you're trimming your locks or your sausage meat, you need a sharp knife and a light touch. To ensure good results, you also need an eagle eye. Start by boning out the birds. Switch to a paring knife and remove the bloodshot meat, plus any raw edges that dried up in transport or in the freezer. You can wash loose blood off the meat without ruining the taste of your sausage. Dried blood, or flesh infused with blood should be cut away.

If you're cleaning out the freezer in August, in anticipation of a new season, you may have to remove freezer burned birds. That fish filleting knife you've been using all summer is the perfect tool to remove the thin layer of freezer burn without taking the healthy meat below. To make the job easier, don't completely thaw the meat you're trimming. Sharpen the fillet knife. Now hold the edge of the knife parallel to the surface of the freezer-burned area, and with a little firmness, cut a very thin slice off the top of it. Many times it's a microscopically thin layer that's been damaged—you can almost see through it. Repeat, if necessary, until all the freezer burn is gone.

Cooking Cased Sausages

For the best-looking cased sausages and the moistest results, my favorite methods of cooking are these two very simple techniques:

In the skillet. Place the cased sausages in a skillet and add enough water to come halfway up the sides of the sausage. Bring the water to a gentle boil, and then reduce the heat to a simmer, cover the pan, and let it simmer about 30 minutes. Remove the cover and let the water gradually evaporate (still at a simmer) as you let the sausages brown slowly. Turn them often to get an even brown. The whole process takes about 40–45 minutes.

On the grill. Preheat your propane or charcoal grill to medium heat and rub a bit of oil on the dog, brat, or wurst. Place on the grill and cook about 10–15 minutes, turning often to make sure all sides get nicely browned. Slice through the thickest end of the sausage and look at the insides to make sure there's no pink left.

As with any game meat, don't overcook these sausages (whether cased or patties) or they'll be dry. Since there's commercial meat in most of these recipes, cook them until the pink is just out. Serve hot as a main course, or better yet, let them cool in the refrigerator, and cut off a slice whenever you need a quick snack.

For those who've never even thought of making their own brats, hot dogs, Italian sausage, and more, here's one last thought to keep in mind. Making sausages is the most forgiving method of cooking game meat. It cures all ills; hides all shortcomings (both of the bird and the shooter); and is a treat anytime of year, for any occasion from appetizers at a holiday dinner to Saturday afternoon barbecues. So dare to use the worst (and the not-so-worst) your freezer has to offer. Then make lots, because these little treasures are going to disappear quickly.

Dogs of a Different Color

Since there's no food dye, and for the most part no curing agent in these recipes, the meat, when cooked, looks a lot like cooked meat—gray or brown. Don't expect bright red hot dogs like the ones you buy at the store; these will be brown when grilled, gray when boiled. If you miss the red too much, add 1 teaspoon Tender Quick per pound of ground meats (both wild and commercial; lean and fat).

Traditional Sage Breakfast Sausage

makes 1 pound of sausage

Ingredients

½ pound pale bird meat
½ pound chicken breast
1 teaspoon dried leaf thyme
2 teaspoons dried leaf sage
¾ teaspoon salt
¼ teaspoon coarsely ground black pepper
1 large egg, lightly beaten

For birds with pale to medium-pale flesh, this recipe is a delicious way to vary the way you eat your game. Who says game meat must be cooked for dinner. Viva breakfast! The only caveat is to grind only meat: no skins or fat are necessary. The fat comes from the egg.

PREPARATION

1. Grind both meats through the coarse plate of your meat grinder and mix thoroughly. Add the thyme, sage, salt, pepper, and egg. Mix again with your hands until the seasoning is well distributed into the meats. Cook a small amount to taste test.
2. Cover and let the sausage sit 24 hours in the refrigerator. Redo the taste test and adjust the seasoning if necessary. Cook it fresh or double wrap and freeze.

COOKING

1. Shape the sausage into 2-inch balls. (A little oil on your hands will make this easy.) In a medium-hot skillet, heat the oil until just bubbling, flatten out the patty until it is about ½-inch thick, and place the sausage in the pan.
2. Cook about 4 minutes a side, until there is no pink inside and the outside is golden brown. Serve with eggs and toast. ❀

Fresh-Mex Breakfast Sausage

makes about 1 pound of sausage

Ingredients

12 ounces dark bird meat
6 ounces side pork
8 cloves minced garlic
4 teaspoons chopped fresh jalapeño peppers (or to taste)
1 cup minced fresh cilantro
½ teaspoon chili powder
1 teaspoon ground cumin
1 teaspoon green pepper Tabasco sauce
2 teaspoons salt
1 teaspoon coarse ground black pepper

A fresh Mexican sausage you can eat any time of the day, cased or shaped into patties. I just like a little spice with breakfast, even when it's not hunting season. Make this sausage with your dark-fleshed birds—even the ones you've been avoiding—or with the palest of the pale. Start making homemade game sausage for breakfasts and you're likely to amaze the family with your versatility.

PREPARATION

1. Grind the bird meat and side pork through the coarse plate of your grinder. Combine the meats with the garlic, raw pepper, cilantro, chili powder, cumin, green Tabasco sauce, salt, and pepper. Mix thoroughly with rubber gloves on your hands. Cook a small amount to taste test, but don't adjust the spices yet. Cover and refrigerate overnight.
2. Repeat the taste test the next day and adjust seasonings if necessary. Stuff in lamb or hog casings, or shape into patties.

COOKING

1. For patties: Pan fry in a medium hot skillet with just a little oil until all the pink is gone (about 10–15 minutes).
2. To grill cased sausages: Preheat the grill to medium heat. Wipe the sausages with a bit of oil, to prevent sticking. Place on the grill, and cook until a warm golden brown on the outside and no pink remains in the middle, about 10 minutes a side. Turn 3–4 times while cooking.
3. For skillet cooking cased sausages: With enough water to rise halfway up the sausages, simmer on low heat for 30 minutes, covered. Then take the cover off, let the water evaporate, and brown the sausages. Turn 3–4 times while cooking.
4. Serve with hash browns, biscuits, and eggs. ◉

Italian Garden Sausage

makes 1½ pounds sausage

Ingredients

1 pound pale meat
8 ounces side pork
¼ cup chopped chives
2 teaspoons minced fresh thyme leaves
2 teaspoons minced fresh sage leaves
2 teaspoons minced fresh basil leaves
1 teaspoon fennel seed, cracked
2 teaspoons salt
2 teaspoons coarsely ground black pepper
4 tablespoons cold water

Every spring when I plant my tomatoes, I think of fall sausages. There's a logical reason. The herbs that go into this Italian sausage recipe are considered perfect mates for tomatoes because they improve their flavor. So plant some basil, thyme, and sage in and around the tomato plants (the chives go with the perennials). Then when you start upland hunting in the fall, make some Italian sausage with your own herbs, tomatoes, and birds. Any pale-meated or mild-tasting bird will work.

PREPARATION

1. Grind the bird meat and side pork through the coarse plate of your grinder. Combine the meats with the chives, thyme, sage, basil, fennel, salt, pepper, and water. Mix thoroughly by hand. Cook a small amount to taste test, adjust seasonings if necessary. Cover and refrigerate overnight.
2. Recheck the flavor the next day.
3. Stuff into hog casings, or shape into patties for cooking.

COOKING

1. For patties: Pan fry in a medium hot skillet with just a little oil until all the pink is gone (about 10–15 minutes).
2. To grill cased sausages: Preheat the grill to medium heat. Wipe the sausages with a bit of oil, to prevent sticking. Place on the grill, and cook until a warm golden brown on the outside and no pink remains in the middle, about 10 minutes a side. Turn 3–4 times while cooking.
3. For skillet cooking cased sausages: With enough water to rise halfway up the sausages, simmer on low heat for 30 minutes, covered. Then take the cover off, let the water evaporate, and brown the sausages. Turn 3-4 times while cooking.
4. Serve with pasta salad and fried zucchini, or cut the sausage up into your favorite lasagna or spaghetti sauce recipe. ❀

Bird Dogs

makes 1½ pounds of hot dogs

Ingredients

1 pound boned dark meat
8 ounces beef suet
2 teaspoons Tender Quick
½ cup nonfat dry milk powder
4 teaspoons dried onion flakes
1 teaspoon ground ginger
2 teaspoons sugar
1 teaspoon sweet paprika
½ teaspoon salt
½ teaspoon cayenne pepper
1 teaspoon white pepper
½ cup cold water

Hot dogs may be the most popular "sausage" in America. So you may want to double, triple, and even quadruple this recipe. Feel free. Use your dark-meated birds for the best results with the beef suet. Anything from doves to Hungarian partridges to sage and sharp-tailed grouse—breasts, legs, and wing meat. Then boil or grill the little doggies. They're delicious either way.

PREPARATION

1. Grind the dark meat and beef suet through the coarse blade of your grinder. Combine with the Tender Quick, onion flakes, ginger, sugar, paprika, salt, cayenne and white peppers, and water. Mix thoroughly by hand. Then run the entire mix through the fine plate of your grinder.
2. Cover and refrigerate overnight to allow the flavors to develop. Cook 1 teaspoon of the sausage mix, cool, and taste. Adjust seasonings if necessary. Stuff in hog casings.

COOKING

1. To boil: Place in a pot of boiling water with enough space in the pot for all the hot dogs to be cooked evenly. When the pot comes back to a full rolling boil, lower the heat to simmer, and cook until all the pink is gone (about 20 to 25 minutes). Cooking time will depend on how densely you packed those hog casings.
2. To grill: Preheat the grill to medium heat. Wipe the sausages with a bit of oil, to prevent sticking. Place on the grill, and cook until a warm golden brown on the outside and no pink remains in the middle, about 10 minutes a side. Turn 3–4 times while cooking.
3. Serve on a hot dog bun or with macaroni and cheese. ✸

Bird Brats

makes 1½ pounds of bratwurst

Ingredients

1 pound dark or light meat
8 ounces side pork
¼ cup cold milk
3 teaspoons dried leaf marjoram
½ teaspoon ground allspice
1 teaspoon dried sage leaves
1 teaspoon salt
2 teaspoons coarsely ground black pepper

Similar to hot dogs but with a bit more European flavor, brats are great grilled, sautéed with potatoes and onions, or simply boiled with beer. Make these from all but the most tender and delicious birds in your freezer.

PREPARATION

1. Grind the meats through the coarse blade of your grinder. In a large bowl, combine the meats with the milk, marjoram, allspice, sage, salt, and pepper. Mix thoroughly by hand. Cook a 1 teaspoon ball of the sausage mix, cool, taste, and adjust seasonings if necessary.

2. Cover and refrigerate overnight to allow the flavors to develop. Taste, adjust seasonings if necessary, and stuff in hog casings.

COOKING

1. To boil: Place in a pot of boiling water or half beer and half water. Leave enough room for all the brats to be cooked evenly. When the pot comes back to a full rolling boil, lower the heat to simmer, and cook until all the pink is gone, about 20–25 minutes. Cooking time will depend on how densely you packed those hog casings.

2. To grill: Preheat the grill to medium heat. Wipe the sausages with a bit of oil, to prevent sticking. Place on the grill, and cook until a warm golden brown on the outside and no pink remains in the middle, about 10 minutes a side. Turn 3–4 times while cooking.

3. Serve with sauerkraut and stone-ground mustard. ◉

Bockwurst

makes about 10 ounces

Ingredients

8 ounces pheasant breast
2 ounces beef suet
2 tablespoons minced yellow onion
2 tablespoons sour cream
1 tablespoon chopped chives
¼ teaspoon ground allspice
½ teaspoon salt
½ teaspoon ground white pepper

I had just turned eighteen and was on The Grand Tour of Europe. Most amazing of all was a white sausage I found in Munich. It was a light and delicately flavored wurst, with just enough sour cream to keep it moist. In other words, the perfect choice for barbecuing some hot evening in the dogdays of summer or for perking up that off-season chill in March.

PREPARATION

1. Grind both meats through the coarse plate of your grinder, twice. Add the onion, sour cream, chives, allspice, salt, and pepper. Mix thoroughly by hand. Cook 1 teaspoon ball of wurst, taste, and adjust seasonings if necessary.
2. Cover and let the sausage sit 24 hours in the refrigerator. Repeat cook-taste test. Case in hog-sized casings. Cook it fresh or freeze it.

COOKING

1. To grill cased sausages: Preheat the grill to medium heat. Wipe the sausages with a bit of oil, to prevent sticking. Place on the grill, and cook until a warm golden brown on the outside and no pink remains in the middle, about 10 minutes a side. Turn 3–4 times while cooking.
2. For skillet cooking sausages: With enough water to rise halfway up the sausages, simmer on low heat for 30 minutes, covered. Then take the cover off, let the water evaporate, and brown the sausages. Turn 3–4 times while cooking. ❂

Tip

To make a very low-fat version of this sausage, substitute 8 ounces of skinned and ground chicken breast for the 2 ounces of beef suet. Keep the rest of the ingredients the same. But don't expect the smooth, creamy texture that good fat provides. This is sausage, after all, and good-tasting sausage needs fat.

Polish Sausage

makes about 1½ pounds

Ingredients

1 pound boned bird meats
8 ounces side pork
1 teaspoon caraway seed, crushed
1 tablespoon dried leaf marjoram
2 teaspoons salt
2 teaspoons black pepper
½ teaspoon ground allspice
½ teaspoon dry mustard powder
¼ cup milk

This Polish sausage is made with side pork, the part of the pig usually brined and smoked for bacon. I've tried making the sausage with the cheaper pork fat, but the consistency of side pork is finer, and makes into a much tastier wurst. For those who are lactose intolerant, feel free to substitute soy milk for the cow's milk in this recipe.

PREPARATION

1. Grind both meats through the coarse plate of your grinder, twice. Combine the caraway seed, marjoram, salt, pepper, allspice, mustard powder, and milk in a small bowl. Add all of this to the ground meats and mix thoroughly by hand. Cook 1 teaspoon of the mix, cool, and taste; adjust seasonings if necessary.
2. Cover and let the sausage sit 24 hours in the refrigerator. Repeat cook-taste test. Then stuff into hog-sized casings. Cook it fresh or freeze it.

COOKING

1. To grill cased sausages: Preheat the grill to medium heat. Wipe the sausages with a bit of oil, to prevent sticking. Place on the grill, and cook until a warm golden brown on the outside and no pink remains in the middle, about 10 minutes a side. Turn 3–4 times while cooking.
2. For skillet cooking sausages: With enough water to rise halfway up the sausages, simmer on low heat for 30 minutes, covered. Then take the cover off, let the water evaporate, and brown the sausages. Turn 3–4 times while cooking. ❀

Oven Salami

makes two 9-inch long salamis

Ingredients

1 pound sage grouse meat
4 ounces beef suet
1½ teaspoons Morton's Tender Quick
4 tablespoons dry red wine
2 tablespoons brown sugar
2 teaspoons dried onion flakes
1 teaspoon onion powder
1 teaspoon garlic salt
2 teaspoons whole mustard seed
2 teaspoons whole coriander seed
2 teaspoons whole black peppercorns

Oven salami is an easy and cheap way to make delicious appetizers and lunchmeats out of your game birds. This recipe is for dark-meated birds like doves as well as gamier birds like sage and sharp-tailed grouse.

PREPARATION

1. Grind the wild bird meat and beef suet through the coarse blade of your grinder, once separately, then together. Add the Tender Quick and mix thoroughly by hand.

2. In a small bowl combine the wine, sugar, onion flakes, onion powder, garlic salt, mustard seed, coriander seed, and black peppercorns. Stir well. Pour this mixture over the ground meats and mix thoroughly by hand.

3. Shape into a roll, about 2-inches in diameter. Wrap in plastic wrap, twist and tuck the ends under and place on a flat plate in the refrigerator. Let the rolls sit overnight to let the flavors mingle.

4. Slice a bit off the end of the roll, cook it, and taste. Adjust seasonings if necessary.

COOKING

1. Preheat the oven to 200°F. Remove the plastic wrap and place the rolls on a cookie sheet. Place in the center of the oven. Bake about 5 hours or until the center is no longer pink.

2. Remove from the oven and let cool until the salami reaches room temperature. Store in the refrigerator up to 4 weeks. To serve, slice thin or thick for sandwiches or with other appetizers for a holiday party. ✸

Smoked Summer Sausage

makes two 6-inch sausages

Ingredients

1 pound sage, dove, or sharptail meat
4 ounces beef suet
1½ teaspoons Morton's Tender Quick
¼ cup milk
6 cloves minced garlic
1 teaspoon salt
1 teaspoon black peppercorns, cracked
½ teaspoon red pepper flakes
6–8 cups apple wood chips

Here's one more way to use your dry smoker and the only way I've found to make homemade hard salamis come out deep red—like the commercial varieties. It is also, by the way, a delicious snacking sausage. Technically, this is what is known as semi-hard sausage, which means you don't need to cook it once it comes out of the smoker. The amount and type of smoke you use is up to you, but my preference is for a moderate amount of chips with a mild fruitwood flavor. Begin here, and you can increase the amount or variety—hickory, for instance, is a much more pungent flavor than apple or cherry—as you wish.

PREPARATION

1. Grind the bird meat and the beef suet through the coarse blade of your grinder, once separately, then together. Add the Tender Quick and mix thoroughly by hand.

2. In a small bowl, combine the milk, garlic, salt, peppercorns, and red pepper flakes. Pour this over the ground meat and mix thoroughly by hand.

3. Shape into a roll about 2 inches in diameter and wrap this in a double layer of cheesecloth or a length of inexpensive deer bag. (Both cotton and synthetic fibers are OK.) Tie off the ends of the sausage with string, leaving one end of string 6–7 inches long. Wrap in plastic wrap and let sit in the refrigerator overnight to let the flavors mingle.

4. Preheat a Little Chief dry smoker, or similar model, with a small amount of apple wood in the chip pan. (Use the small chips only for this smoker.) When you see smoke rising, hang the salami (tying the long end of string to the top shelf and removing the other two shelves so the sausage hangs freely) and close up the smoker.

5. Let the sausage smoke for 8 to 10 hours, adding 6–8 cups of wood chips (one cup at a time) to the smoke pan early in the cooking (about every 30 minutes). When you're done

smoking, take a slice from one end of the roll. There should be no pink in the middle (red, yes—pink, no).

6. Remove the sausage from the smoker and peel the cheese cloth from the sausage. Dry the sausage with paper towels and let it cool to room temperature. It's now ready to eat or to store in a resealable plastic bag in the refrigerator for up to 3 weeks or in the freezer for up to 3 months.

7. Serve thinly sliced for sandwiches or with cheese and crackers. ⊛

The Flavor of Smoke

Two variables control the smoke flavor you get in your food: the essential quality of the wood and the amount you use. Try one of my recipes as written, decide whether you want more or less smoke, a milder or more acrid quality, and you can go from there. My own taste is for a moderate yet distinct smoke that enhances rather than overpowers the seasonings I've used.

The strongest and most popular wood flavor familiar to our American taste buds is hickory, followed by mesquite's distinctive and upright flavor. Milder, and to my taste better, is the mellow smoke of fruit and nut woods like apple, cherry, and pecan. You can also throw other plants into the smoker.

In the last century, willow-smoked goldeye (considered a trash fish by my favorite walleye fanatic) was famous on the Winnipeg Railroad. So famous, in fact, that the lowly goldeye almost became extinct. Harder to get, unless of course you live in wine country, are grape vines. They are like fruit trees in smoke flavor.

Choose which wood's flavor you want, for each recipe; then choose how much or how little of that flavor pleases you. Each time you use your smoker, work at fine tuning this ingredient. And keep in mind what snack foods you buy: if you like smoked foods, use a little more than I suggest. If you don't, then cut back ⅓ to ½ of the wood chips I've suggested.

In the end, it's your choice. That's why we take the time and trouble to smoke our wild game. To get it exactly the way we want it.

Chapter Eight

Field Care

Early-Season Field Care

It's opening day of upland bird season, and in many areas of the country that means warm weather. Shirtsleeve weather at best, miserably warm weather at worst. Trouble is, before we hang up the scattergun and bird vest for the season, we'll be nostalgic for the disappearing warmth of October as we pile on the fleece and fight the age-old battle of gloves vs. unrestricted access to a trigger. In the midst of all this are the birds. Hot or cold, they need to come home in good shape, need to neither broil in the sun nor freeze to the metal bed of the pickup truck. In any weather, field care is the first step to glorious holiday dinners, tender quick-grilled kabobs, and soups and stews that stir the passions and make us count the days until the next opener.

But how do you do it? Starting with the tropical days of the early season, and ending with the last crack of winter sunset light, there are only a few principles to good game care. Depending on how hot or cold the weather is, you have more leeway as to when each step may be completed. At 90°F, game care comes before anything else; at 40°F, a long walk or tossing the birds in the back of the truck for the 30-minute ride home isn't going to cause as many problems. The milder you want the birds to taste (and the more flavorful the bird is originally), the more you need to lean toward these simple rules of warm-weather care:

- Draw the bird as soon as possible. Then wrap the feathers back around the slit you've made to protect the bird from drying out.
- Strong-tasting birds and ones with perforated guts should be rinsed with lots of clean, cold water immediately after drawing. (Sprinkle the insides with salt, too, if "off" smells linger.)
- Put the birds on ice as soon as possible, making sure they cool to about 40°–50°F in the first 2–4 hours after the shot. Then keep the birds cool until you get home.

But how do you implement these principles in the real world, especially when the hunting season may include a hot early September and a frigid late December—often miles from home? The extremes you go to depend on how you hunt.

Initial Care for Stationary Hunting: For hunting birds from a blind or stationary position, initial care is relatively easy. Bring along two coolers with ice: one for your lunch and one for your birds. Then put the bird cooler within reach so you can drop birds onto the ice as soon as you have them in hand. (If there's no shade for the cooler, bury the birds in the ice.) No need to draw the birds in the middle of the shooting. The cooler the weather or the more game flavor you want, the longer you can wait to draw them. Conversely, the warmer the weather or the less flavor you want, the faster you'll want to draw the birds. But don't go longer than 2–4 hours before drawing the birds, even in coolest weather.

Initial Care for the 1–2 Hour Walk or Loop: In warm to moderate weather, carrying birds in your game vest (tucked in against your back) will not only keep you warmer but will prevent the birds from cooling down. It is therefore a good idea to keep a cooler loaded with ice in your vehicle, and circle back regularly to drop the birds in.

Initial Care for the Long Walk: Sometimes there's no other way to get into an area. You drop a vehicle on each end and walk until you're done walking. On cold or cool days, draw the birds within a couple of hours of the kill; they should start cooling down over the course of your walk. But on warm days, there are a couple of options. Take advantage of the new vests with bird pockets that hang away from your body. And carry several frozen water bottles in your game pocket. We recycle 12- to 16-ounce plastic pop bottles for this purpose. Just half-fill the bottles with water and place them upright in the freezer. (Be sure they're propped up that way, or they'll tip and the ice will block the mouth of the bottle.) Once frozen, top off each bottle with water and slide them into the game pocket of your vest. As you walk and hunt, the ice melts gradually, keeping the water—as well as you and your birds—cool. (For hotter weather, fill some of the bottles completely before freezing them.)

Cooler Stuffing: If you're hunting more than an hour from home, you need to carry clean water, coolers, and lots of ice. In our truck, there's a 5-gallon jug of water just for cleaning birds. We also keep two coolers, each set up the same: a block of ice on the bottom (because it lasts longer) and a bag or two of cubed ice on top. (If your cooler is small or you need more room for birds, you'll have to forego the block of ice.) Once we have birds to cool, the cubed ice gets broken up and the birds buried in it. That's the advantage of cubes: they conform to odd, round shapes and, consequently, cool the birds down faster.

More than a handful of birds? Try stacking. Start with a 2- to 3-inch layer of cubed ice in the bottom of the cooler, then place a single layer of birds across the ice. Lay an inch or two of cubed ice among and across the top of the birds. Add another layer of birds, and finally, a layer of ice across the top. Every bird should be surrounded by ice.

Running out of room? Start a second cooler. It can take 6 hours or more to go from almost 100°F (a bird's body temperature) down to 40°F—even in a cooler. As long as the birds retain any body heat, which can be as long as 6 to 12 hours, you want to keep them layered in ice. Don't rearrange them to save space. Don't open the cooler. Once the birds cool down to 40°F you can consolidate them, stacking birds against each other, side by side, with ice on top and bottom. And to keep them from swimming in the inevitable ice melt, put the cooled birds in resealable plastic bags. (Large ones, with capacities of 2 to 3 gallons, will hold 6 to 8 quail or 2 whole pheasants in the feather.)

The Truth About Coolers

Some bird hunters are lucky enough to own a piece of bird cover right outside their back door. Get lucky, the bird is back in the kitchen in 20 minutes. For the rest of us, coolers are still an essential piece of equipment for making sure birds get and stay cool on the drive home—be it 2 hours or 2 days. Maybe you should take another look at that essential piece of equipment. Are you still depending on that cooler you bought during the early 1980s, when you had more time than money and were looking for the cheapest big cooler you could find at the discount store?

Maybe that was OK when you were in your twenties. But maturity and perspective should lead you to the logic of spending a few more bucks for a cooler (or two) that's actually insulated enough that you don't have to stop every 12 to 24 hours for ice.

I came to this revelation some time ago, about halfway from Michigan to Montana on a 90-degree afternoon, with 6 sage grouse, 12 woodcock, and 5 ruffed grouse in the cheap discount cooler in the back of my vehicle. Despite three bags of ice above, between, and below the birds—and throwing as much air conditioning into the back of the vehicle as I could—the ice was melting faster than the miles.

Back home, with the birds safely in the freezer, I looked at my options for buying coolers:

- A cheap discount store cooler with friction fit lid, about $20.
- A heavy-duty cooler with 2 inches of insulation all around, including the lid. Some even come with a metal-clasp lid that seals the cold in and the hot out, about $75 to $100.
- The thermoelectric cooler that plugs into your cigarette lighter or, with an adapter, into a power outlet in your motel room, about $110.

Being a dyed-in-the-fleece baby boomer, I was immediately drawn to the thermoelectric models. Imagine, driving down the road with my own personal bird refrigerator. No wasted time stopping for ice. No wasted space in the cooler for ice. All birds—every square inch.

But, hold on boomer, these marvels have a downside, too. A thermoelectric cooler is rated to reduce the temperature inside the cooler to 40°F degrees below the ambient air. That 40°F is also the temperature at which you want your birds held. That means any time the temperature in the car gets above 80°F—including when you stop for the night and turn the air conditioning off—your birds will get too warm. Worse yet, if you leave the cooler hooked up to your parked vehicle overnight, with the engine off, you might just wake up to a dead battery. On the other hand, if you stay at a facility wired for electricity, you can plug in the thermoelectric cooler indoors. In a 75-degree room, the cooler would operate close to the same temperatures maintained by your refrigerator at home. This also means lugging the cooler in and out of motel rooms each morning and evening.

At that point in my deliberations, I remembered that the cooler we'd taken on the recent hunt was the one we'd bought at a drug store for less than $25. I didn't have a clue where—or what—the insulating factor was. I also remembered how much I hate dead batteries.

So I bought a pair of high-quality, nonelectric coolers with a lid that has 2 inches of insulation. They are capable of keeping ice for five days at 90°F. I'm still stuck with the ice taking up valuable space, but I don't need as much ice, nor do I have to stop as often to replenish it. Oh, and keeping my own personal maturity in mind, I got a cooler with wheels and a long handle. It's a Coleman Xtreme. The 54-quart stainless steel cooler will set you back approximately $100). It works anywhere the birds fly, costs less than your ammo, and my heirs will probably fight over it. If you buy the camo model, you can easily take it into the field with you.

How To Use A Cooler

The rules of the road with all coolers are pretty basic. No matter what the brand or price tag, the ice—and cold—last longer if you:

- Don't open the lid often. If you must open it, don't keep it open long.
- Keep the cooler out of direct sunlight: ice lasts at least twice as long in the shade.
- Keep it full with ice and birds. Dead air takes more energy to cool.
- Prechill the cooler. Before you take that bird walk, place a bag of cube or block ice in the cooler. Overnight is best; an hour or two is OK.
- Don't drain cold water from the cooler. Just-melted ice is almost as cold as the ice itself and certainly colder than the ambient air. Drain only when reorganizing the cooler, when the water turns warm, or when adding new ice.
- Keep one cooler just for the birds. Put beverages, lunch, snacks, and things you need to get at several times a day in a separate cooler.

Preliminary Drawing

Warm or cold, once you come to a stop you need to consider drawing the birds. Because I like mild wild flavors, I draw all birds in the field (or within the first hour of the kill). At first, this is just a drawing of the intestinal tract—stomach, and small and large intestines. And because I like moist birds, I make as small a hole as possible, either with a small gut hook (see sidebar on page 145) or a pocket knife.

For Relatively Undamaged Birds: To draw birds with a gut hook, insert the hook into the vent. Rotate it a bit, so as to hook the gut, and begin pulling, gently but firmly, back out of the vent. Once the intestines start coming, grab hold with your fingers, and continue pulling, until all the intestines, large and small, and the stomach have been removed.

To draw birds with a knife, lay the point of the knife at the vent and make the first cut downward to the tail (not up toward the breast). With some birds, and some hands, this is enough and avoids the risk of tearing the breast skin. Then slide your index finger—or your pinky, for smaller birds—into the chest cavity and hook it on the lower end of the large intestines. Draw gently but firmly, and the rest of the intestinal tract should follow. (Leave the gizzard for later.) If the birds are eating vegetation exclusively, there's no need to pull the craw yet. If, however, they've been eating insects, remove the craw now.

Once the bird is drawn, check to see that there's nothing but feathers and skin at the vent. If even a vestige of the intestinal tract remains, trim it off. Now tuck the feathers back around the vent, and put the bird on ice until you're ready to complete the processing at home.

For Damaged Birds: In the process of doing the field dressing, I'm also doing a minor autopsy—mostly to check that there are no perforations of the intestinal tract. If the tract is whole, the milder tasting birds need no further field work. But if any of the intestinal tract has been punctured, you need to rinse the cavity with enough clean cold water so that it runs clear, and there are no unpleasant odors inside. After a good rinse, if you smell any intestinal odor, sprinkle some salt in the body cavity: 1 teaspoon for small birds, up to 2 tablespoons for a mature sage grouse or turkey.

For Stronger Tasting Birds: I also like to rinse strong-tasting birds right after the preliminary drawing. Sharptails, sage grouse, and prairie chickens improve greatly with a good cold rinse after drawing. Mature birds of these species also get a sprinkle of salt: 2 teaspoons for the smaller birds, 2 tablespoons for larger ones. Early-season young-of-the-year birds don't always need salt, but if they smell gamy on drawing, or if the guts are punctured, salt them anyway. Leave the salt inside about 24 hours, then rinse it out with copious amounts of cold running water. If the insides still smell a bit sour, give it another dose of salt and let it work in the refrigerator overnight, then rinse again.

Finally, if it's hot enough to wish you had air conditioning in the camper, stuff ice cubes inside the larger birds (such as pheasants, sage grouse, and turkeys) to help them cool down faster. All birds then get buried in an ice-filled cooler. The lid should be shut tight, the cooler placed in as much shade as possible.

High vs. Mild Flavor: If you prefer stronger tasting birds and "high" flavor, hold off drawing until after the aging process. Hang the bird by the neck in a cool, shaded bug-free place. For the most flavor, do as the English do—leave the bird hanging until the body falls from the neck. A friend of mine swears by this method, and claims that pheasants, for example, absolutely can't go bad no matter how long you hang them this way.

I admit I've never had the guts to eat pheasants at his house, but I've eaten birds hung this way in other, unavoidable, situations. They were not to my liking. But taste is an individual and quirky thing. What you bring to the table should be what you enjoy eating, not what someone else tells you you should enjoy.

If you think all wild birds are gamy, and either give all your birds away or seriously dread eating them, it may be worth your while to change your game-care technique. I push all my game animals as far as they can be pushed toward the milder side of the flavor spectrum, and despite Mother Nature, these methods generally accomplish that.

Gut Hooks

Why is a gut hook better than a knife? It's a question of proportions. The chief complaint people make about eating wild birds is that they are dry. There are three reasons they get that way: (1) Mother Nature made them that way, (2) over-cooking, and (3) opening the bird so wide to draw it that the meat is exposed and dries out either on the trip home, aging in the refrigerator, or in the freezer. The same thing happens when you breast and skin the bird in the field, of course, and that is reason enough to leave the feathers on until you're ready to cook or freeze the bird.

The smaller the cut in the bird's vent, the less the interior is exposed to air. When drawing the bird without a gut hook, at a minimum you need to make a finger-sized cut. Since the vast majority of hunters are men, that often means a sizeable hole in a sometimes very small bird. On a turkey it hardly matters. On doves, woodcock, Hungarian partridge, or quail it is monumental. Using a gut hook allows you to draw the bird's innards through a much smaller hole (⅜ inch at most) so the meat will stay moist, and your hands stay cleaner in the process. If the intestinal tract is intact, you're done. If you spot perforations, open the bird enough to rinse it out well.

Be sure to choose a bird-sized gut hook, as most are made for big game.

Gut-Shot or Not Gut-Shot

There's no mystery to figuring out if a bird's been gut-shot. Just eyeball the intestines as you draw the bird. If they're not smooth and clean (clean being a relative term here), they're fine. Take a whiff of the insides of the bird. Be warned, however, that some birds always smell sour, and not always the ones you'd expect. Woodcock, for instance, smell great, while ruffed grouse are pretty dicey. What you're looking for is a whiff of intestinal smell, nothing else.

Curing Mistakes

Salt is also a good cure for neglected birds of any variation. Last spring I hunted at a lodge. Through a series of miscommunications, one of my birds didn't get drawn—until I got home. Things looked—and smelled—pretty grim, but I went ahead and cleaned the bird, rinsed it vigorously, trimmed away damaged skin and meat, and heavily salted the inside of the body cavity. I let it sit in the refrigerator 24 hours, then put the bird in the freezer—without rinsing the salt out. We ate that bird last week—four months later. The meat was delicious, tender, and not the least bit gamy or sour. (Eventually, the salt percolated down into the pan juices, without effecting the flavor of the meat at all.) The bird? A turkey. I was going to eat that bird no matter what, but it was a huge relief that it tasted so good.

Ordinarily, we would only leave the salt inside about 24 hours, then rinse it out with lots and lots of cold water. If the insides still smell a bit sour, give it another dose of salt and let it work in the refrigerator 24 more hours, then rinse again.

Parting Birds In the Field

What if you are more than a few hours from home and have too many birds to fit in your cooler? The most practical solution is to part out the birds—that is, pluck or skin them, cut the legs from the breast and, if necessary, take out the bones (more on this in the next chapter). You'll lose some moisture because feathers keep skin from drying out, and skin keeps meat from drying out, but you can at least cool all the birds and prevent spoilage. Once parted out, pack the birds loosely in resealable plastic bags, with a few drops of clean water in each bag. (Plucked birds can still be aged when you get home, inside the bags. Boned birds, not as well.)

If you do start stripping your birds, remember to leave the required proof of sex and/or species attached until you arrive at your permanent residence. That proof may be a wing or spurs, naturally attached. Check the regulations of the state you're hunting in.

Beware The Gift Horse

If you're hunting with an outfitter or at a lodge, your host will usually take care of basic field care, as well as plucking, cleaning, and flash-freezing birds. Be sure you know exactly how your host is going to take care of your precious birds. Some will always skin and breast out birds. Others always pluck and draw. Still others have methods of their own. Recently my husband hunted pheasants at a lodge in eastern Montana and took the lodge up on their offer to care for the birds. What a surprise when we opened the packages at home. All the birds had been neatly plucked and drawn—no problem. But instead of separating the wing at the joint (either shoulder or elbow), they had broken the humerus (upper arm bone) midlength with a cleaver. I'd heard of this being done with geese but never with pheasants, and it's a perfectly ridiculous thing to do with any bird. Why? Because it leaves sharp, jagged bones that will puncture any freezer wrap and cause freezer burn. What if you plan to eat the birds right away? Chew carefully because there will be a side order of sharp bone chips.

Check the services a lodge or outfitter offers and get details on how bird preparation will be done from the people who will do the actual work. The only reason to pay someone else do the work is to not have to do it yourself. If their work only leads to more work for you, why waste the money?

Cold-Weather Field Care

It may come as a surprise, but in very cold weather (not a 20–30°F day, but one so cold your eyelashes stick together) your birds can freeze within 2 to 4 hours of being shot. When it is that cold, a process called cold shortening makes meat tough, and no amount of aging, marinating, or cooking will cure it. This is true whether you started out with very young or very old birds, though with very old birds you may only be adding insult to injury. It's the young ones you don't want to ruin.

To prevent cold shortening, keep the birds from freezing during the first 36 hours after they've been killed—a time when they are still stiffened with rigor mortis.

At 0–10°F ambient temperature, a good way to maintain birds at an optimum temperature of 35° to 45°F is to put them in an insulated cooler with a tight-fitting lid (without ice). In even more extreme cold weather, move the cooler inside the passenger compartment, as far from the heater as possible. Throw a little ice on the birds and if they are not starting to cool down in 2 to 3 hours, load your cooler with ice just as though it were a hot day. It's a bit more trouble, but your birds will be more tender.

Whether it's hot or cold weather, it's a good idea to check on your cooler during the first cooling down period. If necessary, rotate the birds so they cool properly without freezing. Then shut the lid and keep it shut so the cooler can maintain the proper temperature.

Aging Birds

While most of the upland birds you bring home in the course of a season will be the young of the year, even those birds are older and tougher than commercially raised chickens (the average commercial chicken is only some six weeks old). Later in the season the birds you shoot will be older still, and occasionally you'll deliver to your table a big ol' bird that has lived for more than one year. (According to biologists, the average winterkill is about 60 percent for all wild birds.) I don't like trusting my luck when it comes to game care, so I age all birds, young or old.

The refrigerator is the best and safest place to age wild birds since you can set the controls for a constant temperature: refrigerators are normally 35°F at the top and 38°F at the bottom. I age all game birds for 7 to 8 days on the bottom shelf at 38°F.

Here's the order of unpacking when we return from a hunt: the dogs, the bird coolers, everything else. And before "everything else," the birds are transferred from the coolers to the fridge. Somewhere after that comes a shower, a beer, and dinner.

We place the birds in plastic bags, one or two to a bag, and if they're still warm, rotate them occasionally (top to bottom and back to breast) to cool evenly. Plastic bags should be closed tight. Modern frost-free refrigerators dry out birds, and the plastic bags will help keep moisture in. On the slim chance that your refrigerator is old enough to not be frost-free, you can use paper bags.

My friend Tim has converted a small refrigerator (with the freezer compartment inside it) for aging birds. He took out all but the top shelf, inserted S-hooks on the rungs of that shelf, and hangs birds there.

If you don't have a second refrigerator or spare room in the main refrigerator, you'll need to find a cool, bug-free location. An unheated, shaded garage or a basement will work, as long as it stays consistently between 35° and 45°F. Lay your birds on the cold concrete or hang them from the rafters for 5 to 7 days; if the birds are still warm at first, be sure they don't touch. Five days is enough at 45°F. At any temperature, keep a close watch. And don't age birds, if the average daily temperature (night and day) is not below 50°F. While the birds are hanging, check them morning and evening, sniffing them and testing the back feathers for ease of plucking. When the back feathers pluck easily, the bird is usually done aging. Always err on the side of caution. It is better to eat a slightly tough bird than throw one out because it has spoiled.

Complete the Drawing

If you did the preliminary drawing in the field, you still have a little work to do. Start by opening the drawing hole (cutting toward the tail, not toward the sternum) as little as you can, but enough to reach all the way into the body cavity.

Now is the time to remove the crop if you didn't remove it in the field. Rinse any crop spillover from the breast meat. Remove everything that isn't hard bone or healthy muscle (diaphragm, lungs, heart, liver, esophagus, etc). Feel along the hard inside of the rib cage and spine, to make sure you've got it all. Now run clean, cold water through the cavity until the water runs clear on the other end. Double check: Wad up a single paper towel and rub it along the length of the inside of the rib cage and spine. It will pick up the last bits of blood and tissue. Then rinse again. Trim up any rough edges, then dry the bird inside and out with paper towels.

First Aid For Bloodshot Meat

At some point during your hunting season, no matter how far ahead of the beak you shoot, you're going to place a few pellets in the breast meat we all prize so highly. The problem isn't just the pellets: it's the blood. Blood, no matter what the animal, the cut, or the dish, will add a bad flavor to your dinner. It's important to remove it, and to remove it in a way that doesn't waste meat.

One way to do it is to slice the meat across the point of penetration—deep enough to remove the piece of shot—and then carefully trim away any bloodshot meat. Another way is to soak the meat in brine before wrapping and freezing. In truth this is just another marinade. Chefs in many gourmet restaurants use an overnight soak in very cold brine solution to make their commercially raised "wild" birds taste less wild and cook up moister for their nonhunting customers. I learned it from an avid pheasant hunter who treated all his birds this way. I prefer to treat only bloodshot birds—ones I've had to skin and bone—with brine, while aging intact birds in the refrigerator. But my friend Arnie, who showed me this method, prefers all his birds, shot up or intact, to be brined. Here's how to do it:

Skin and part out the birds, boning the breasts and separating the legs from the carcass at the hip socket. (For specifics on parting out birds, see pages 154–157.)

- Remove any shot pellets and bloodshot meat.
- Rinse the breasts and legs in cold running water.
- For large batches of birds: Fill a 5-gallon plastic pail or ceramic crock about two thirds full with very cold water and add approximately 3 tablespoons of table salt; stir to dissolve.
- For small batches of birds: In a plastic, glass, or ceramic container, add 2 teaspoons of salt for each gallon of cold water.
- Place the brine container in the bottom of your refrigerator; if you're using the 5-gallon bucket, place it in an unheated garage. In either case, the temperature should be near freezing. (The mild brine solution should not freeze even if the air temperature is a bit below freezing.)

- Place a chunk of ice enclosed in plastic in the top of the bucket. You can freeze gallon milk jugs full of water for this purpose; even if the ice melts, there's no possibility of diluting the brine, and the jug keeps the birds submerged.
- Let the brine work overnight and then remove the breasts and legs, rinse again in cold running water, air dry, and wrap for the freezer.

Neither the salt put inside the carcass after preliminary field dressing nor this brine soak adds much salt to the meat. Sprinkling salt inside the bird merely draws out blood and other impurities inside the body cavity so they will not penetrate the meat. The brine soak is fairly weak. I'm quite salt-sensitive, but I don't taste the salt in the cooked birds nor do I then delete the additional salt called for in the recipe. However, the heavy salt marinade I describe in Curing Mistakes on page 145 is used only for meat that would be inedible otherwise; if it is successful in removing all objectionable odors, then you should cook the meat without additional salt (and toss out the pan drippings).

Chapter Nine

Plucking, Skinning, and Parting Out

The Best Time to Dry Pluck

Plucking an upland bird simply isn't the chore that it is with waterfowl. Although the easiest time to pluck any upland bird is when it first hits the ground, in truth, nearly all upland birds are reasonably easy to pluck any time after the kill, including after freezing (more about that later). The exceptions are ruffed, blue, and Franklin grouse, which have breast skin that is incredibly easy to tear whether you pluck immediately after the kill or after aging 5-7 days. With such thin skin you wonder how they survive winters in the North Country. Thank goodness they do.

Dove and woodcock feathers are so easy to pull that most bird dogs would classify them as self pluckers. Pluck them in the field or that evening, or wait 5–7 days as they age. It doesn't matter. Pheasants, Hungarian and chukar partridge, quail, and prairie grouse (sage and sharptails) are best plucked right after the kill. Next best is after aging the birds as mentioned above. Third best, you can choose to pluck them after rigor mortis has gone out, which can be anywhere from 24–36 hours later, depending on the weather.

There's even more good news: upland birds (excluding the thin-skinned grouse) can be plucked as easily after they've been frozen as they can before freezing. If you don't have the time to pluck them all at once before freezing, you can still draw the birds, age them a few days, then freeze them in feather in a double layer of resealable bags. You can then pluck the birds leisurely as you use them. The upside of this method is that feathers are as good as any other protection against freezer burn. The downside is that whole, feathered birds take up more room in the freezer.

One trick to dry plucking once-frozen birds is to thaw them completely before you start plucking. It will make the job much easier, and if, like me, you have a little arthritis, your hands will appreciate the warmth.

Freezer time should still be limited to about six months, even with the feather insulation. Before wrapping, arrange feathers to cover all the skin; exposed skin will freezer burn. (Do not, however, carry this practice over to waterfowl. Freezing only sets duck and goose feathers, making them impossible to pluck.)

Wet Plucking

There's a third choice for upland hunters. You can pluck a frozen bird and refreeze it without harming the meat. Of course, there's a trick, but since a fellow upland hunter shared it with me, I'll share it with you.

I learned this method from an avid pheasant hunter who happened to be seated with me at a wildlife benefit dinner. After a day in the field, he said, he often lacks time to pluck the birds, so he freezes them (with the stomach and intestines drawn) in the feather. Then over the next week or two, as time allows, he pulls out as many birds as he has time to pluck. Instead of taking the time to thaw them in the refrigerator (24–48 hours depending on the size of the bird), he dips one or two at a time in a pot of not-quite-boiling water (about 180°F) for 1½ to 2 minutes. The goal is to thaw the skin, and the skin only. Then he sets the birds on newspaper until they're just cool enough to handle (about 2–3 minutes more) and starts plucking. When he's done, he double wraps the birds (first in plastic wrap, then into a resealable plastic bag) and pops them back in the freezer, still 85–90 percent frozen.

There are many advantages to this system. First, you don't have to pluck all your birds right after you've spent a strenuous day or two hiking the hills and valleys. You don't even have to pluck them until the bird season is over, when you really do have a breather.

Second, you don't have to plan 24–48 hours ahead to allow frozen birds to thaw before plucking them. (Life isn't always that predictable.) With this method, you can pull two birds out of the freezer and only be committed to those two birds. Have more time? As you start plucking the second bird, pull out a couple more and swish them around in the hot water.

Another advantage to wet plucking is that the feathers don't fly nearly as far and wide as they do when dry plucking. As a result, you can pluck indoors on a winter day without having to hire a maid service.

My generous dinner companion did light up when I suggested that he could have put those birds in the bottom of the refrigerator to age, and then plucked them anytime during that period. But sometimes even that 5- to 7-day aging period isn't enough time. After all, bird seasons last for months, and 5–7 days may mean you've only traded one busy hunting weekend for the next. As long as the birds have their intestinal tract removed first, they are perfectly safe in the freezer with a layer of feathers and double plastic bags for insulation.

A Word About Plucking Grouse

I know ruffed grouse are Kings of the Hill, Sultans of Sauté. But to the person who's stuck plucking their royal breast, they're mighty thin-skinned, as are their royal cousins the blue and Franklin grouse of the mountains. I'd rather pluck a brace of pheasants any day. To pluck any of these grouse without tearing the skin takes infinite patience. Start with the back, wings, and legs; you'll get the hang of plucking and if you make a mistake it won't show as much as on the breast.

Now turn the bird over on its back. One by one, ever so carefully, pull each breast feather out as you gently but firmly press the index finger and thumb of your opposite hand around the base of the feather to protect the skin from tearing.

Plucking and Parting Out Birds

WHOLE, SKIN-ON BIRDS

Once plucked, you can choose to leave the bird whole, or you can part it out (cut it up) into breast and legs. The photos on the next few pages provide tips on plucking and parting out birds, as well as some finer points of preparing birds for the table.

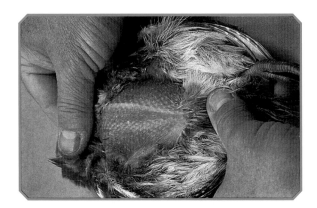

1. Place the bird on its back. Starting at the belly, with the bird's feet firmly in your off hand, pluck the feathers of the lower breast.

2. Pinch a few feathers between your thumb and index finger and roll or pull them gently but firmly in the direction they're set. With the feet in your hands, you'll see the breast feathers are set so they pull toward you. If the feathers pull hard or the skin is delicate, reduce the number of feathers taken in each pull. (Anything to keep from tearing the skin.) Pluck down to the thighs and drumsticks.

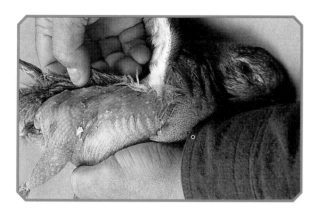

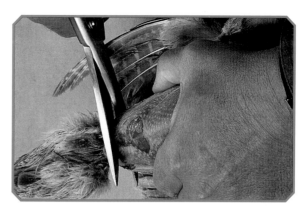

3. Holding the bird on its side, pluck along the side and back of the torso. Pluck down to the tail feather assembly in back. Don't pull the tail feathers.

4. When you have plucked the feathers down level with the bottom of the pelvis, cut the tail section off. Cut cleanly; this will open the body cavity so that later you can clean and rinse the bird easily. With the tail feathers out of the way, return to the legs. Pluck as much of the leg as you want to keep (or whatever your local fish and game department requires; regulations often require you keep only the thighs, but since there's so little meat on the smaller upland birds, I leave the lower leg, or drumstick, attached as well).

5. Bend the ankle joint (it's at the bottom of the drumstick) back hard enough to make the bones pop through the skin.

6. With a knife or poultry shear, cut through the ligaments at the ankle. Cut cleanly between the long bones of the leg so that there will be no sharp edges to puncture freezer wrap and no bone fragments to eat. Pluck the upper wing down to the elbow joint.

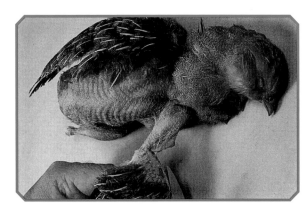

7. With the wing stretched out and your shears parallel to the lower wingbone, cut though the loose skin at the elbow joint. Bend the elbow back so that the joint pops open, exposing the ends of the upper and lower wing bones.

8. Clip between the bones with your poultry shears. No sharp edges, no loose bone chips. Cutting between the long bones of the wing leaves a smooth, safe bird for the freezer and table. The extra skin you plucked makes for an attractive appearance.

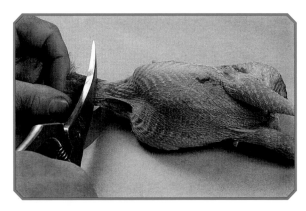

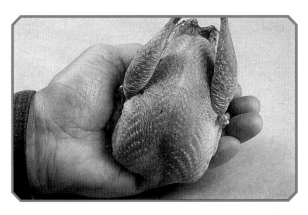

9. Pluck the feathers halfway up the neck to the head. Stretch out the neck and cut through spine, skin, and tissue. Carefully push the skin down from the neck tissue, and cut through the neck bone and tissue again (but not the skin) close to the breast. For small birds, a good chef's knife or poultry shears will cut through easily. For larger birds, use poultry shears. And for turkeys, use either a cleaver or gardening shears. Smooth the extra flap of skin over the neck opening.

10. The extra time you spent plucking halfway up the neck and cutting twice leaves a neat, attractive bird for the table—not the ragged effect that one cut leaves. Take a kitchen torch or a candle and singe the last wispy feathers.

11. Finish drawing the bird. Preliminary drawing in the field took the intestinal tract, but now you need to remove the crop, esophagus, lungs, and the rest of the internal organs. Wipe the inside of the bird with a wadded paper towel, rubbing along the rib cage and along the spine to loosen any stray tissue. Now rinse with cold water. The water should run clean and clear through the opened body cavity. If not, run your fingers inside the body cavity again. Rinse and repeat.

12. The Turkey Variation: Despite the vastly different size of turkeys compared to almost any other upland bird, their skeletal structure is the same, so parting out is also the same, except for one small procedure: you need to neatly cut off the beard.

Quick and Dirty: Skinning Whole Birds

1. Begin with the bird on its back. Pluck enough breast feathers so you can get a pinch of skin, then slice through the skin.

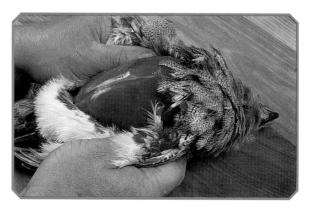

2. Slide your thumb under the skin and pull the breast skin gently but firmly from the muscle. The goal is to take the skin cleanly without tearing the meat. Pull smoothly and slow down if necessary.

3. Note that the crop is still attached. Skinning and parting in this method, if you do it soon after the kill, eliminates the need to draw the bird. (If you're planning to age the bird first, draw the intestines in the field as usual but leave the crop intact.)

4. Pulling smoothly on the lower breast skin, expose the legs. Pull the skin down over the feet. Repeat for the other leg. Once the legs are free, pull the breast skin farther to expose the shoulder joint.

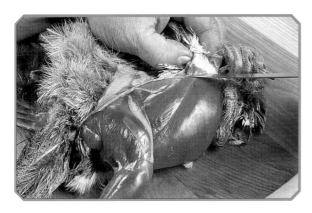

5. With a sharp paring knife, slice between the humerus (upper wing/arm bone) and the ends of the shoulder blade and wishbone. They come together here and are held only by ligaments and tendons. With the wings gone, continue pulling the skin off the carcass, moving toward the backbone from both sides.

6. Holding the tail firmly, pull what little of the hide is still attached to the back, pulling from tail to the head.

7. With poultry shears or a knife, cut off the tail feather assembly below the pelvic bones. (It's a fatty, easy-to-cut appendage hanging off the skeleton.) If you haven't drawn the bird, cutting below the pelvic bones will also keep you from perforating the intestines.

8. Press the thigh against the back, popping the top of the femur (thigh bone) out of the hip socket. Slice through the ligaments holding the leg to the hip. Repeat for the other leg. Set the legs aside.

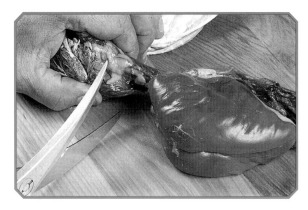

9. Pull the skin over the head, exposing the neck. With a chef's knife, poultry shears, or garden shears cut through the neck just at the top of the breast.

Anatomy of A Skeleton

The only trick to taking birds apart—whether you are boning birds or removing broken bones—is to keep their anatomy firmly in mind. Birds are not much different from humans: bend their knees, elbows, or shoulders the wrong way, and the same ligaments and tendons get hyper-extended. Just remember how your joints work properly and apply that backwards when taking birds apart. Knees, for instance, are meant to bend back. Bent up and forward, you can easily create enough space to slide a pair of poultry shears through and make a clean cut between the bones.

Work methodically. Start at the breast and then, in turn, work on the legs, wings, back, neck, and tail assembly.

Parting It Out

BONE-IN BREAST

Take the breast section in one hand. At this point, the back and ribs are still attached and need to be removed. Starting at the lower breast, clip through the soft tissue attached to the sternum. Using the hard edge of the sternum as guide, cut away the ribs from the sternum. Clip around one side until you come to the shoulder joint. You have already removed the wingbone, but now you need to separate the other two bones that make up the shoulder joint to free the sternum from the back. This is where the scapula (shoulder blade) meets the clavicle (the collarbone in humans; wishbone in birds).

1 & 2. Feel for the joint where the clavicle and scapula butt up against each other (at the top of the shoulder). Slide your knife or poultry shears between the ends of these bones and clip through the ligaments. Repeat for the other side.

3. Rinse the back of the sternum. When you're done, there should be no loose pieces of bone, tissue, or internal organs left—only the inverted cup of the sternum itself with breast meat attached.

BONED-OUT BREAST

At our house, we've discovered that upland birds tend to suffer more damage in the shooting than waterfowl. My guess is that there are two main reasons for this: upland birds have less feather cover than waterfowl, and upland hunters tend to use smaller shot and more numerous individual pellets. I mention this now because this is where we deal with all these pellet impacts and try to save as much meat as possible.

This Hungarian partridge was hit several times in the breast. There's still quite a bit of usable meat, however, if you bone it out and use it in recipes that call for diced meat. This is also a very popular and quick way to handle undamaged birds.

New Math, Again

The breast of any bird includes both pieces of meat filleted from the sternum. In other words, it's a case of one and one equaling only one. In this book, as in all cookbooks, anytime the breast (singular) is called for, it means both sides taken from one bird.

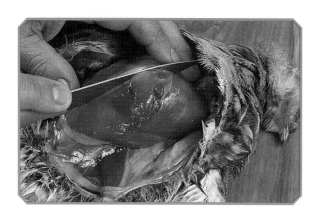

1. To bone the breast, pull enough skin to give you room to work. Start your cut at one side of the top of the sternum. As you work, think of yourself as scraping the meat from the bone rather than cutting it off the bone.

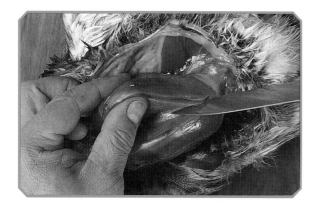

2 Place the bird on a cutting board, feet toward you. Keeping the back of your knife hard up against the bony ridge of the sternum, slice down one side of the sternum. Once you've cut partly down the breast, pull the boned meat to one side so you can see better and scrape along the length of the sternum. Continue to scrape the breast meat from the center of the sternum down to the rib cage as you move down toward the foot of the sternum. Now turn the bird so the head is toward you. Place your knife against the sternum and run it up toward the head until you feel the wishbone (clavicle). You've seen lots of wishbones. It's actually two bones: both left and right clavicle (or collarbones). In humans, the clavicles are separate and lay flat across the top of the chest; in birds, with their deeper and narrower rib cage, they're joined into an arch, sitting like a doorjamb astride the base of the throat.

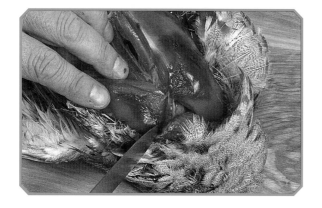

3. Place your knife against the wishbone, at the top of the arch, and run it down the length of the bone to the shoulder joint.

4. Slip your knife under the wishbone and free the breast meat attached to it. Depending on the size of the bird, this can be a fair-sized nugget that is often tossed out with the carcass. With the breast meat free of the wishbone, continue to scrape the breast from the rib cage. Work your knife down the side of the chest cavity.

5. Lift the breast meat off the rib cage as you work, cutting it free from the skin and carcass. Almost free: working back up toward the shoulder joint. Note how little meat is left on this side of the carcass. You can see the entire length of the sternum, the wishbone, and even the thigh below.

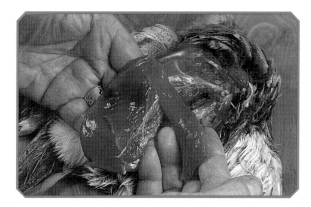

6. At the shoulder, free the last corner of meat from the carcass.

7. The boned breast as seen from the underside. Note the loose flap of muscle. You've seen this in commercially raised and wild birds if you cook a lot of boned breasts. This loose flap is called a tenderloin. In all birds, it is the most tender part of the breast.

There is a quicker way to remove the breast-sternum in one piece. A lot of quail hunters simply stretch the breast skin tight with one hand, then perforate the body cavity with the other thumb. Holding the wings back, they then press the thumb up against the inside of the sternum (breastbone) and snap the sternum up quickly. Done well, I hear, you have a clean, easy job of breasting a bird. I've never mastered the technique nor have I been lucky enough to see it done well. So I continue to use poultry shears for the best table look.

Damage Control

Whether you freeze in paper or plastic, or throw the bird on the grill right after it has been shot, you need to check for broken bones. Splintered bones and bone fragments perforate freezer wrap and allow freezer burn to destroy your treasured birds. Munching around bone chips is no fun either.

If your shot was too centered or the bird not far enough away, it's best to bone the bird out. But if it's a matter of a broken leg or wing, a little careful knife work will keep your bird essentially whole.

1. **A perfect bird, except for an obvious broken lower leg.**

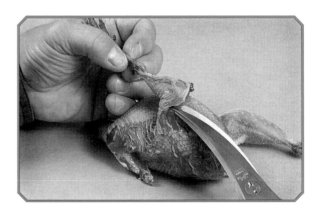

2. **To remove the damaged lower leg bones (there are two: the tibia and fibula), first cut through the break, exposing the lower leg bones, and picking out the chips carefully. Trim away the muscle to expose the knee joint.**

3. Bend the knee joint back to expose the ends of the lower and upper leg bones.

4. Cut between the bones with your shears. Now you have a bird that's not dangerous to eat.

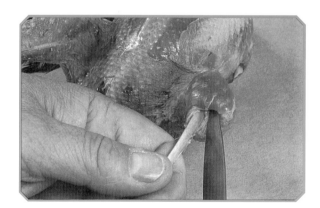

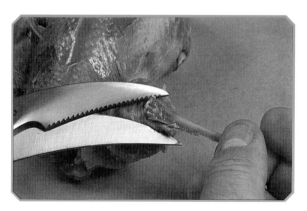

5. To remove a damaged upper leg bone (femur): Cut through the damaged part of the leg, exposing the femur. Slide your paring knife along the length of the femur, freeing it from the meat. Continue up the leg until your reach the hip socket.

6. Bend the femur back against the hip joint, then gradually slice through the ligaments that hold the femur in the hip socket. Remove the femur. If the bone has been splintered badly, be sure to look for bone chips before you wrap the bird.

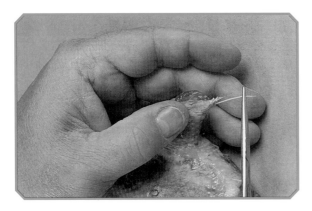

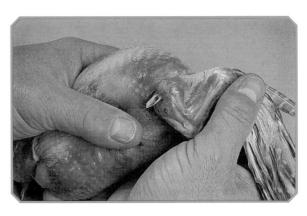

7. On older birds that tend to have tough legs, including pheasants, remove the leg tendons. They're the hard, white, skinny things sticking out from the knee joint. (The older the bird, the harder the tendons.) Grasp the end with a hemostat (borrow it from your fly vest or buy one at a fly shop) and pull gently but firmly.

8. To remove the upper wingbone (humerus): Feel for the broken bone and push the sharp, jagged edge through the skin where you can see it.

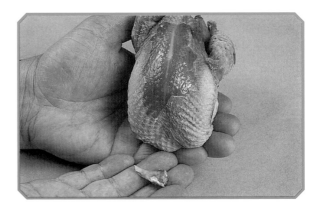

9. Clip the wing just below the break. Slide your shears along the humerus, between muscle and bone, up to the shoulder. Pop the shoulder joint out by pressing it backward against the body. Clip through the tendons and ligaments that hold the shoulder in.

10. Remove the humerus and check for bone splinters.

The Hatchet Job

Sometimes it's not the shot itself that causes damage to the wings. For some people, including some field dressers who work for lodges and outfitters, the standard procedure for larger birds is to whack the humerus (upper arm bone) in half with a meat cleaver.

Since bones never break cleanly, you'll end up with bone chips in the meat and a jagged edge to the bone that will perforate your freezer wrap and let freezer burn destroy perfectly good birds.

If you use a hatchet on wings, STOP! If you end up with birds treated this way, follow these directions for removing the rest of the humerus.

Taking the Bird Apart for the Grill

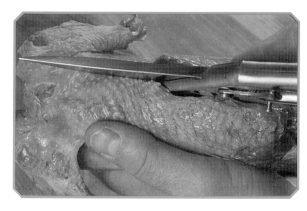

1. Once the bird is plucked, you can make it lie flat on the grill by removing the backbone. Hold the bird in your hand breast down, feet toward you. With your poultry shears, cut along the right side of the spine, keeping as close to the spine as possible to avoid wasting meat. Keep your shears parallel as you cut to the neck opening. You'll be cutting through the ribs, which are pretty thin.

2. Do the same with the left side of the spine.

3. Remove the spine from the bird and throw it away. Or save it for stock if you make your own.

4. Place your thumbs inside the carcass and press on the shoulder joints on each side and push back so the upper wing folds up into the breast. This pops the upper wing bone (humerus) out of joint.

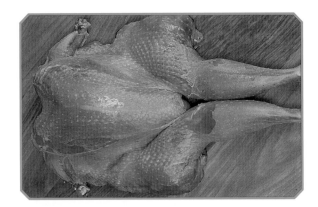

5. The whole bird will now lay flatter on the grill. Because of the thickness of the meat, choose a recipe that uses indirect cooking over a medium (350°F) fire to ensure good results.

6. For hot grilling birds larger than doves, you will have better results if you take the bird apart further. Start by cutting through the skin that connects the thigh to the breast. There's no hip joint anymore, so you can do this easily with knife or shears. Keep your knife close to the top of the leg bone, so you'll have lots of skin to cover the breast while cooking.

7. Now you can cook the legs and breast separately.

One More Trick

Often the problem with wild birds is that they're so small that serving a grilled breast is not very dramatic. The easy way to solve that is to remove the sternum (breast bone) while leaving the two halves as one. Here's how.

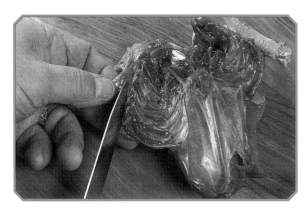 

1. Start with a de-spined bird with the breast skin-side down on the cutting board and the inside of the sternum and rib cage facing up. Place your paring knife under the ribs, between meat and bones, and lift the ribs off the breast meat.

2. Lift the ribs, moving toward the center of the breast until you get to the sternum itself.

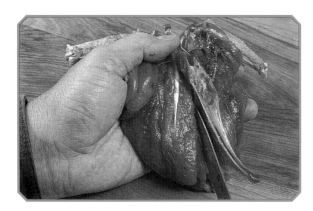 

3. Slide your knife between the sternum and the breast meat, scraping the meat away from the sides of the bone. When you've finished scraping the meat from each of the breastbone, lift the sternum up off the meat and carefully use the paring knife to free it from the breast meat, bottom to top.

4. Work as close as you can to the bone so little meat is wasted.

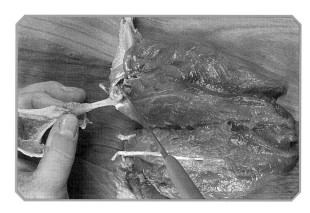 

5. Eventually you'll get to the shoulder joint. Lift the sternum and you will see the exposed joint. Slice between the ends of the bone, through the tendons and ligaments that hold the shoulder together.

6. Legs and really flat breast, ready for the grill—or any other cooking method you have in mind. The real joy of this method is that all of the small bones are now gone and you can quick-cook a fairly large piece of meat instead of the tiny half-breasts you get from boning the traditional way. Not for every night perhaps, but certainly worth the effort for special occasions.

One More Breast Trick

Don't want to go through the trouble of removing the sternum? Why not just cut through it? With a good pair of poultry shears or a cleaver with a real steady hand, this is the easiest way to have your bones and grill them, too. Start with a whole bird, legs and all. Each piece will be ½ a bird.

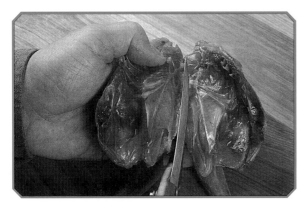

1. Pluck the bird and remove the backbone. Turn the breast down in your hand and start cutting through the sternum at the bottom. Small bites at a time if you have to, but cut up the middle of the sternum in as straight and centered a line as you can. Use both hands if needed.

2. Then clip through the wishbone at the top of the breast. (You can do this with any upland birds except turkeys. Don't try it with ducks and geese. Their wishbones are much thicker.)

Good Bye Dry, Chewy Legs

Just because you want to dry roast your birds, doesn't mean the legs have to be DRY roasted. Put them in the tuck position to make your bird a nice tight package.

1. Cut a small slit through the skin on either side of the pelvis. Gently bend the leg at the knee and slip it through the hole.

2. The legs will stay tucked while cooking, protecting them from oven heat, and will be more moist and tender at the table.

Chapter Ten

Wrapping and Freezing

Wrapping the Birds

Now that you've plucked your good birds, removed broken bones from the damaged ones, and salt-soaked the ugly ones, you need to wrap them for the freezer. The goal here is to prevent the freezer's cold, dry air from reaching the bird and causing freezer burn. For best results, use the best wrapping materials available, press the air out carefully, and organize your freezer so packages don't get tumbled, damaged, and lost.

Then again, don't let your birds linger endlessly in the freezer. Plan to eat your game birds within 6 months after freezing. You can keep them after that, but, depending on how well they're wrapped and how well your wrapping job holds up, your birds may lose a bit of flavor and texture, as well as begin to show signs of freezer burn.

Here again, the great variety in upland birds complicates the matter.

For small upland birds—quail and chukar all the way up to Huns and sharptails—the best way I've found to store whole birds is to double wrap them in plastic, or to freeze and then vacuum seal them. Larger upland birds—sage grouse and whole turkeys—lend themselves to plastic under paper. Parted-out birds can be wrapped in any of these three ways.

As you're wrapping, keep in mind the size of your family and how much protein they eat at a meal. Also keep in mind that the larger the package—and the smaller the outer surface compared to the whole package—the less area can be damaged from freezer burn. So pack skinned breasts in as large and closely packed a pile as you can logically use at one sitting. Here are a few other options for wrapping that vast pile of birds in your freezer.

In individual packages:

- Sort birds by species.
- Sort birds by parts: breasts into one bag and legs in another.
- Sort birds by toughness: tough legs or tough birds can be packaged together for a multispecies slow-cooker recipe or other special handling.
- Sort birds by taste: If you don't have a lot of each species, similar-tasting birds can be used very well in the same recipe. But do keep track of toughness. Put tender pale birds, with tender pale birds; tough dark birds with tough dark birds.

To avoid a rough-and-tumble search-and-destroy mission, divide your freezer into sections and make a map. We usually divide the freezer into six major sections: in half lengthwise and in thirds across.

This year birds are taking up the left third of the upstairs freezer: pale-meated birds are in back; dark-meated birds are in front; and each species in its own brown paper grocery bag, clearly marked.

Big game is in the middle section: steaks and burger in front; roasts and stew meat in back (short- versus long-cooking). The right front is fish; right rear is garden stuff and miscellaneous. Turkeys are in the downstairs freezer so they don't get disturbed or their packaging damaged by frequent intrusions.

I once tried keeping a tally of individual birds, but like keeping a diary, that lasted about 3 weeks. The map works and it is easy to keep up to date. If you only have one freezer, you can put your Christmas turkey in a little-used corner, mark it on the map so you don't go there accidentally, and it will be fresh and unspoiled when you pull it out for the holidays.

Let's define terms: the three most effective methods are double plastic wrap, paper and plastic wrap, and vacuum sealing.

Double Plastic Wrap: Start with a good quality plastic wrap—a piece at least four to five times longer than the bird or bird parts you are wrapping. Covering the package three times doesn't hurt: plastic wrap is cheap, freezer burn disastrous.

Wrap each bird separately, tucking the legs and wings firmly against the carcass as you wrap. Roll the bird along as you go, and press the air out. Tuck the ends snugly against the body. Secure the wrap with masking tape, sealing all loose ends. Now drop it into a resealable freezer-weight plastic bag and label it (e.g., species, whole bird, breasts, legs) and date it. Press the air out of the freezer bag and seal.

Paper and Plastic Wrap: This is an inexpensive and effective method of wrapping large whole birds or compact packages of boned meat. This is how we wrap boned turkey breasts and whole turkeys.

For boned-out meat: Cut a piece of plastic wrap at least four to five times the size of your portion of boned meat. Place the meat in the center of one end of the wrap, then roll up the meat, pressing the air out to the sides and folding the sides over to form a tight, air-free envelope. Tape down the ends with masking tape. The result should be a solid rectangle, similar to a package of deer steaks or burger-no odd corners, no big air pockets. Cut an equal length of freezer paper, center the meat at one end of the paper and roll, pressing the air out to the sides; fold the sides over the package like an envelope. Tape, label, and drop into the freezer.

For whole birds: First, accept the fact that you're not going to succeed in making a neat, airless package. If nothing else, the inside of the bird will provide enough air to give freezer burn a good head start. So either look ahead to the section on vacuum sealing or plan on eating the bird within 1 to 3 months.

Start with about 18 inches of plastic wrap. Holding the drumsticks firmly against the body, tightly wrap the plastic twice around the lower body, trapping the legs and closing off the lower body cavity opening. Now cut another piece four to five times the length of the bird. Starting near the neck opening, wrap the bird as tightly as you can, pressing the wings against the carcass and pushing air out ahead of the wrap. Make sure there are at least two layers of wrap over the entire bird. If not, cut one more piece to wrap and cover the places that still need a double layer. Tape the ends down. Now cut a length of paper about three or four times the length of the bird. Set the bird in the middle of the paper, at a diagonal. Take one end and wrap it across the top of one shoulder and down the breast; tuck this end under the bird. Fold the paper over at the neck opening, creasing and folding it, to conform (as well as you can) to the shape of the bird. Continue to fold, crease, roll, and wrap the bird until it is completely encased; tape tightly around the legs. Press the paper against the carcass as tightly as possible as you (or a friend) wrap tape around the bird. Use lots of tape—it's cheap. You should end up with a package that looks like a bird—with at least two layers of paper and two layers of plastic on all surfaces.

Tape all loose ends, label the bird as to date and species, and place it in an out-of-the-way spot in your freezer. Keeping movement to a minimum will ensure that those odd angles and corners won't come loose—or worse yet, tear—during storage. (I've even been known to add a final layer of bubble wrap to large birds.)

Vacuum Sealing: Vacuum-sealed foods last three or four times longer in the freezer without freezer damage. They provide better protection against freezer burn and turning the little fat that's in upland birds rancid. To vacuum seal effectively you need a high-quality sealer with heavy bags. I've tried a couple of vacuum seals, and for my money, the best is the FoodSaver brand. If you don't process more than 20 packages at a time, the manual, less expensive models are quite sufficient. Larger models are better suited to high-volume users.

This is my first choice for birds pheasant-size or smaller that I want to freeze more than 3 or 4 months and for birds I've parted out into breasts and legs. The process is the same no matter what you're sealing.

The first step is to "dry" the birds so that moisture doesn't get vacuumed into the seal—and abort the seal. There are two ways to do this:

- Wrap breasts, legs, and whole birds in plastic wrap to trap the moisture. Vacuum seal.
- Arrange your whole or parted birds on cookie sheets and set them in the freezer. At 0°F, the moisture will be solid in about 3 hours. Process one package to test. If the moisture doesn't start running up the package into the sealer, they're ready. If you're sealing whole birds, first dry the insides with a paper towel, before placing in the freezer. Once frozen, vacuum seal.

At our house, we prefer to freeze the birds because it's less work, and we get a dinner break between the processing and the sealing.

A Food Saver vacuum sealer costs more than a roll of plastic wrap, but it has certain advantages. For one thing, being able to see the meat through the vacuum wrap makes it easier to decide what's for dinner. You'll know at a glance not only species and cut, but whether that breast looks good enough for company. Plus vacuum-sealed packages take up less room, lie flat, and give birds more protection against freezer burn.

My second favorite use of the vacuum sealer is to prepackage my own home cooking. Over the years, we've worked out an almost mess-free system, preparing our own "frozen boil-in-bag" dinners. If there's a motel available, we bring a microwave. In the camper we bring a large pot to boil water in. No more restaurants and their chicken-fried steaks with instant mashed potatoes and institutional brown gravy. No more eggs swimming in grease and half-raw hash browns. Plus we save money, and spend more days afield hunting our beloved birds.

Freezing Your Birds

Now, to the freezers. To get the best texture and flavor from your birds, you need to freeze those birds fairly quickly. According to the experts, at 0° to -5°F, your freezer will safely and efficiently freeze about 1½ pounds of food per cubic foot of space. So if you've got a 15 cubic foot freezer, plan on freezing no more than 22 pounds of birds at any one time.

There are a couple of other things you can do to help your freezer:

- Don't toss all the warm, recently wrapped meat into a box or a bag and put it into the freezer. Distribute individual packages on top of or among the frozen packages already in the freezer.
- Take advantage of the hanging wire baskets that come with your freezer. Whole birds or large packages of meat freeze faster in baskets.
- If you need to layer, place packages on metal cookie sheets. Stack the sheets using already frozen packages at the corners to space them. Layers should be just high enough to allow cold air to circulate around the new packages.
- If you've got more than one freezer, spread the wealth. You don't have to push the 1½-pound limit. The faster it freezes, the better the texture and taste.
- Check on your birds 24 hours later. Everything should be solid. If you're not quite there, rotate and move packages around to get the cold where it is needed.
- And it wouldn't hurt to throw a refrigerator-freezer thermometer in your freezer(s) an hour or so before you're finished processing. Adjust the freezer to 0° to -5°F if necessary, before adding the warm birds.

The State of Your Freezer

Even with the best of wrapping technique and technology, if you store you birds in an inefficient freezer, you'll shorten their freezer life significantly. And when I say freezer life, I'm not talking pie in the sky—I'm talking dinner.

Which freezer is best? The chest freezer, bar none. Optimal temperature for storing any food is a constant 0 to 5°F. The chest freezer not only operates at that temperature with the door closed, it stays at that temperature for several minutes with the door open. Because the door is on top, the cold does not drop out as soon as you open it.

We all know that heat rises and cold sinks. Every time you open your upright freezer, the cold drops out into your heated kitchen. Since nature abhors a vacuum, warm kitchen air quickly rushes in to replace it. If you're contemplating a new freezer, buy a chest freezer.

If you have an upright, open it as little as possible. When you do, take out enough meat for 1 to 2 weeks at a time, and transfer it to the freezer compartment of the fridge. It won't suffer much in 2 weeks, and the rest of your stored treasures will be comfortable in a constant blanket of cold air—without the constant tropical breezes. The best place for an upright freezer is in an unheated basement where the air is usually only 50 degrees warmer than the freezer.

I once timed my freezers, setting thermometers in all three, then watching to see how long it took for the temperature to rise. My refrigerator's upright freezer compartment rose as soon as I opened the door. I gave up on the two chest freezers: four minutes and counting with nary a degree difference. Same initial cost, same size, more efficient. It doesn't get any better than that.

Reversing the Process: Thawing in the Microwave

Thawing birds is almost as delicate a process as thawing fish, if you want to keep the meat moist. The trick is to do it slowly, letting the bird rest between defrost cycles. And check for warm spots: If you feel even the smallest warm spot, let the bird sit 10 to 20 minutes until it cools off. For birds the size of chukars, usually just under 1 pound, I set my 700 watt microwave on thaw (or defrost), which gives me about 250 watts. I thaw the bird for 2 minutes, let it sit 5 minutes, and thaw for 2 more minutes. After that, I do a lot of touching and use no more than 15-second increments of defrosting. Generally, a total of 4½ minutes of processing with this stop-and-go method is plenty to thaw out a 1-pound bird.

Smaller birds take less time, larger birds more—but the process is the same. Thaw, rest, thaw, feel. Then back off if the edges start to warm up. For safety's sake, limit the total time to about 30 minutes. And remember that unless you are deep frying the bird, it doesn't have to be totally thawed before you start cooking. (For deep frying it's a safety issue: trapped ice particles will splatter badly when they hit the hot oil.)

Everything but a whole turkey—which is best thawed slowly in the refrigerator—can be thawed in the microwave.